THE MAINE
HOUSE

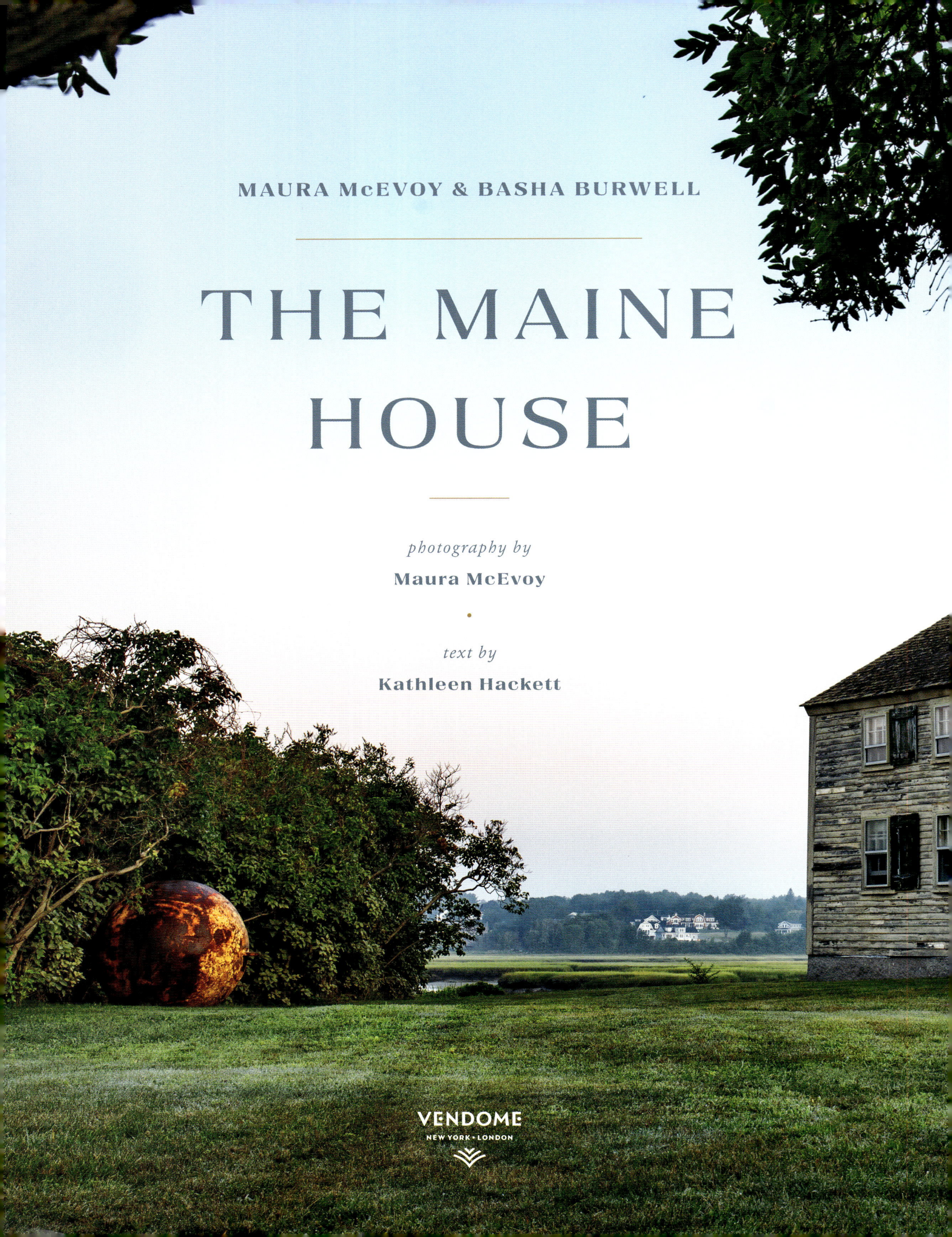

MAURA McEVOY & BASHA BURWELL

THE MAINE HOUSE

photography by

Maura McEvoy

•

text by

Kathleen Hackett

VENDOME
NEW YORK • LONDON

CONTENTS

INTRODUCTION

"Maine is an opportune place, particularly if you are worried about life in America today, if you think that the people who are running things have lost touch with the truth that is taught by the land."

Richard Saltonstall Jr. wrote those words in his seminal work, *Maine Pilgrimage: The Search for an American Way of Life*, after traveling through the state for three years, registering and documenting the environmental concerns facing its people, and offering solutions that underscored a need for cooperation between man and nature. The year was 1972.

Maura McEvoy was about six years old when Saltonstall's book was published, right around the time that the Army Corps of Engineers installed a jetty on the southern Maine beach where she spent every summer of her childhood in her grandparents' cottage, which is still there. Erected to protect a handful of boats, the jetty sucked away the white sand beach and replaced it with rocks. Soon thereafter, multiple nearby classic cottages were demolished to accommodate a motor inn. The inn was followed by a condominium complex that scarred forever the sunset view from the beloved family cottage.

The path E. B. White walked every day to his writing shack (see pages 142–49).

Maura remembers feeling the destruction viscerally. She recalls the chatter among the adults in the room. "Why are we always changing everything?"

It is a question that stayed with her as, summer after summer, change gained a stranglehold on the place she loved more than anywhere else in the world. But it would be decades and a thriving career before Maura combined her two loves—photography and Maine—in an effort to preserve the version of her Maine that was swiftly vanishing. Her mantra would make a great bumper sticker: Maine is not a teardown.

When the idea to turn her lens homeward struck, Maura called Basha Burwell first. Her family—on both sides—dates back multiple generations in Maine. Basha spent her formative years on the coast, running between Grandmother Fran's big old colonial house and Nana Dede's summer cottage overlooking Harraseeket Harbor. The cottage, built in 1911—the same year as Maura's grandparents' place—is the last remaining real summer cottage in the village. From a young age, Basha learned the beauty and value of preservation and conservation from her father, who never let convenience and expediency get in the way of honest restoration; he renovated their homes with his own hands, always eschewing the newfangled for the architecturally correct. It was an apprenticeship that led to her career as a creative director and stylist—and a knowledge of special Maine houses gained over years of being a gentle trespasser.

For four years and over 3,000 miles, Maura and Basha traveled throughout Maine, traversing dozens of fingers of land, ferrying across bays and reaches, braving dubious dirt roads, and strolling seaside towns in search of what the artist Jamie Wyeth once described as a quality of life that is singular and unique. They often arose at 5 A.M. to capture a sunrise and the ethereal mist suspended over a harbor. They peeked inside sloping barns and behind boat sheds, under hundred-year-old eaves and over one very beautiful balcony (page 205). One of their first forays was to an island where they had devised an ambitious schedule for themselves. So when Bill Alcorn, whose home sets a high bar for the mythic Maine house (pages 22–31), loaned them his ancient Citroën for the day, they

OPPOSITE: An iconic view, through an iconic window.

took him up on it. Any plan to quietly make their way around a place where everyone knows everyone went out the window the minute Basha got behind the wheel of the finicky French car; its temperamental stick shift, the spotty GPS, and dubiously marked roads would have made a great silent film if they weren't laughing so hard. Generosity followed them everywhere. When it became clear that they weren't going to make a ferry, Sharon and Paul Mrozinski graciously opened up their charming attic bedroom (page 269), fitted out with camp cots and the most indulgent French duvets.

Maura and Basha made all kinds of plans—and learned firsthand what Nadja Zerunian, who opened her home up to them (pages 116–23), meant when she said Maine is all about the weather. It was terrible about 75 percent of the time, but they did not have the luxury of waiting for better days. Both have full-time jobs and coordinated the shoots in the margins. They did what people in Maine do: accepted it and took the best from it.

On some days, the light was so perfect that Maura would walk around with her camera, feverishly shooting out of hand, moved by the way a chair, railing, porch, or painting was illuminated. It is Proustian, that light. It takes her straight back to her grandmother's cottage, where as a teenager she photographed the same old chair in the basement over and over, so moved by the light streaming in through the tiny window there. Basha invariably responded to spaces that recalled those glorious childhood years spent between the grandmothers: the smell of old pine, mildew, moth balls, cedar, and line-dried linens. She knew instinctively when not to touch an interior, and in fact did so very infrequently. Rather, she relied on a lifetime of Maine memories to frame it up just so.

With each house Maura and Basha visited, two or three more suggestions inevitably followed. At an early point, they were advised to create a narrative around what a Maine house meant, but both resisted, too curious and open to commit to a definition too soon. Their compass? They kept the dial on "we know it when we see it." In the end, there were dozens that didn't make it into *The Maine House*, but they easily could have.

OPPOSITE: Sunset at Bill Alcorn's saltwater farm (see pages 22–31).

Eventually, the two realized they *did* need a narrative. And that's when they called Kathleen Hackett, a native New Englander whose ties to Maine are bound in the Mid-Coast, to a tiny village home just around the corner from her sister. Hers is a Maine of mountains and sea, of salt air and pine, of ship captain's houses and fishermen's shacks. To get to write about E. B. White's writing shed (pages 142–49) would be especially poignant; as a child, she checked out *Charlotte's Web* from her local library sixteen times.

Our hope is that *The Maine House* serves as both a record of and a tribute to the place we all want it to be, the one that plays out in a city-dweller's fantasy, a child's dream (cue Robert McCloskey's *One Morning in Maine* and *Blueberries for Sal*), an artist's imagination (as rendered by the likes of Alex Katz, Louise Nevelson, Katherine Bradford, Fairfield Porter, Neil Welliver, Lois Dodd [pages 172–83], and Andrew and Jamie Wyeth, to name a few), a sailor's aspirations ("I cannot *not* sail." —E. B. White), and a nature-lover's reverie.

To that end, we made choices. Here are houses created by the people who live in them, distinctive for their ingenuity, originality, and fierce individuality. Here are spaces that personify the artists whose work is made better through struggle, a Mainer's point of pride. Here are cottages resolutely unchanged—where to silence a slamming screen door would be to strip the place of its soul. Here are warped floorboards and lovingly worn camp sofas sat on by generations of the same family. Here are homes where a life well lived is defined by spirit, creativity, and longevity. Here is a kind of visual wealth that money just can't buy. Here is *The Maine House*.

Maura McEvoy
WELLS, MAINE

Basha Burwell
BROOKLIN, MAINE

Kathleen Hackett
ROCKPORT, MAINE

OPPOSITE: A pied peacock at Tony Elliott's Snug Harbor Farm (see pages 276–85).

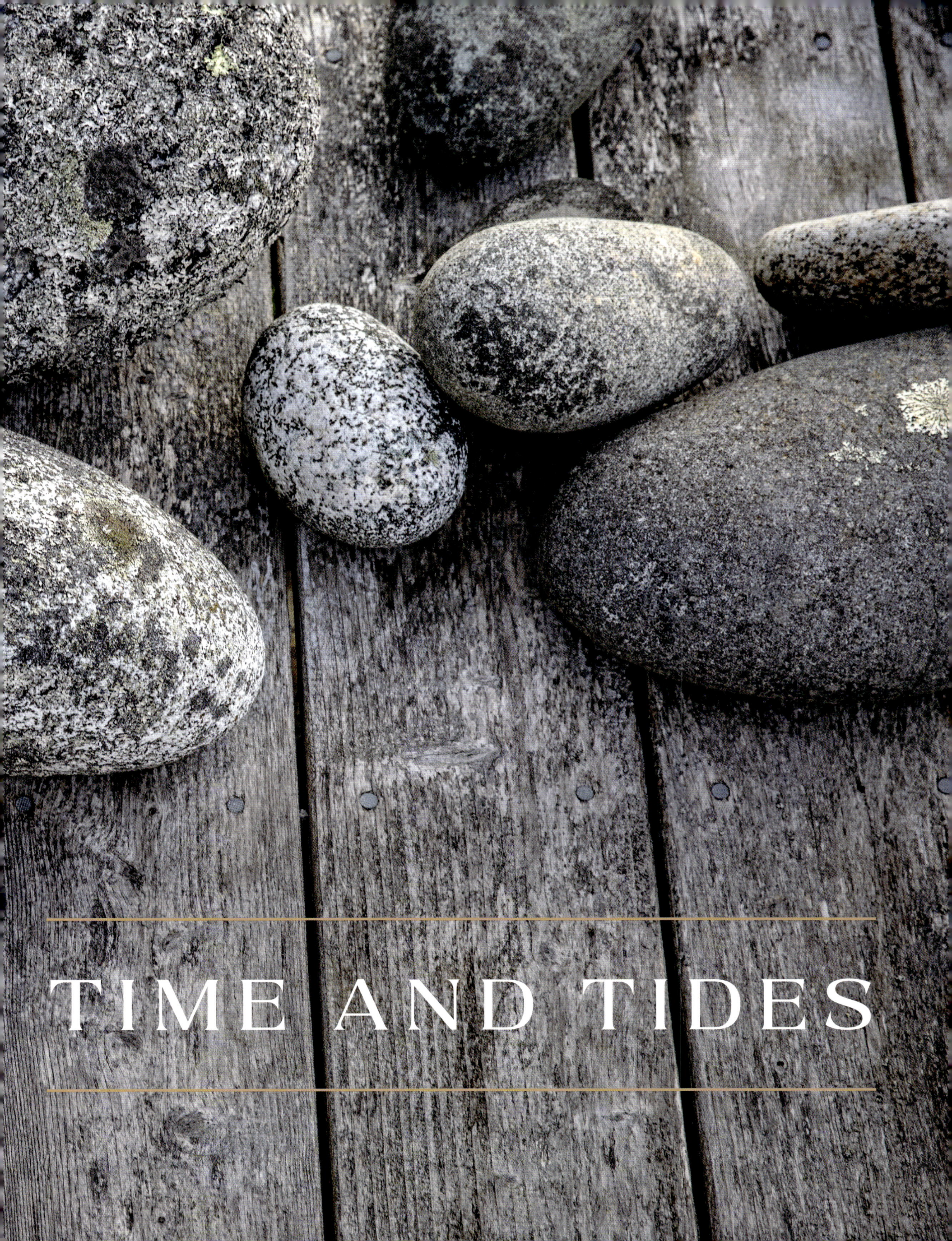

TIME AND TIDES

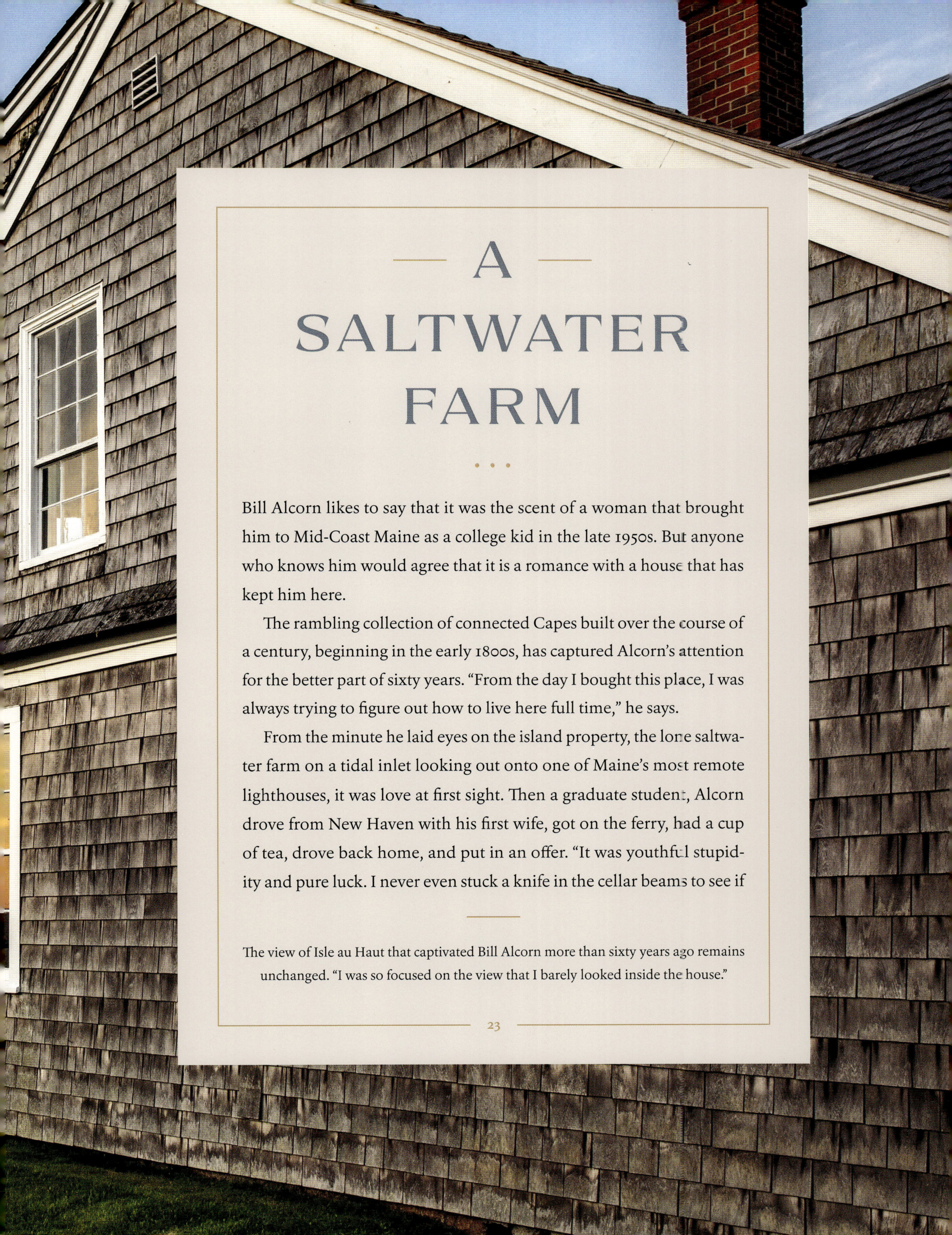

A SALTWATER FARM

Bill Alcorn likes to say that it was the scent of a woman that brought him to Mid-Coast Maine as a college kid in the late 1950s. But anyone who knows him would agree that it is a romance with a house that has kept him here.

The rambling collection of connected Capes built over the course of a century, beginning in the early 1800s, has captured Alcorn's attention for the better part of sixty years. "From the day I bought this place, I was always trying to figure out how to live here full time," he says.

From the minute he laid eyes on the island property, the lone saltwater farm on a tidal inlet looking out onto one of Maine's most remote lighthouses, it was love at first sight. Then a graduate student, Alcorn drove from New Haven with his first wife, got on the ferry, had a cup of tea, drove back home, and put in an offer. "It was youthful stupidity and pure luck. I never even stuck a knife in the cellar beams to see if

The view of Isle au Haut that captivated Bill Alcorn more than sixty years ago remains unchanged. "I was so focused on the view that I barely looked inside the house."

they were any good. I didn't go into the barn at all. It was just such a beautiful spot," he says. So what if there was no electricity, a hand water pump in the kitchen, and an outhouse?

It's been two decades since Alcorn solved the riddle of residing full-time in his beloved island idyll. There have been upgrades, repairs, and sensitive renovations, the last one to level an egregiously sloping floor. "I really just wanted to jack up the existing floor, but I realized it was going to rip the whole thing apart," he says. Instead, he installed a new one and left the ceiling at a tilt.

Like any successful relationship, there is continual give and take between property and owner. And lucky for this house, Alcorn is reluctant to change too much of the place he fell for all those years ago. "I remember the real estate agent saying it needed a lot of love. So that's what I do, I give it a lot of love."

ABOVE: The house gradually expanded over a century, with the oldest portion, far left, built in the early 1800s. OPPOSITE: Clad in a mix of cedar shingles and clapboard, the rambling farmhouse features some of its original small-paned windows; others were replaced with the two-over-two style in the 1900s.

OVERLEAF: There's no need for an alarm clock when Maine light streams in through unadorned bedroom windows.

OPPOSITE: A windowed door frames a view as if a companion painting to the one on the adjacent wall. ABOVE: A twin bed set on a simple slatted frame fits snugly under one of the house's many eaves. An old lobster trap, turned on its side, serves as a bedside table.

LEFT: A colorful stash of crab-trap bait bags hangs in the barn.

BELOW: A former outhouse with a glorious view is now a storage shed.

OPPOSITE: A tire swing rests on a beam, out of the way of Alcorn's flat-iron skiff, the accomplished boatbuilder's latest project.

Maura McEvoy

BACK OF THE MOON

• • •

I have spent every summer of my life in southern Maine, in the same house where my mother—and her mother and father—spent their Julys and Augusts. The modest shingled cottage, caught on a slip of land between the ocean and a mile of tidal marshes, has stood, season after season, through some of the harshest weather the East Coast can dish out. With the exception of an indoor shower, an upstairs toilet, and some double-paned windows, it is unchanged since it was built in 1911.

Whenever we gather there, my siblings and I play the lottery game. As in, "What would you do if you won the lottery?" My answer is invariably the same: I would rescue every house on the street from being torn down and replaced by a McMansion. I have not yet won the lottery, but it felt like I did a few years ago when the owners of a cottage three doors down decided to sell.

The aluminum siding didn't deter me. Nor did the knob-and-tube electrical wiring, the camper toilet upstairs, the layers of carpet and linoleum, or the inexplicable layout—the best views were from the bathroom. I ignored all that and marveled at the intact 1920s interior. The view of the marsh was the best I had ever seen.

I looked at old photographs for inspiration, and realized that the guiding design principle more than a century ago focused on being outdoors; who cared if the kitchen window faced the neighbor? No one was going to be

A stretch of modest cottages along my southern Maine beach has survived the rampant development that surrounds it.

BACK OF THE MOON
172

OPPOSITE: I replaced the aluminum siding with classic cedar shingles, which weathered to a pleasing gray quickly, thanks to the proximity to salt air.

LEFT: The house's original wood siding was left untouched on the interior wall of the sun porch.

OVERLEAF: The original kitchen faced the house next door; I re-sited it to take advantage of a view of the tidal marsh.

spending much time inside anyway. I figured out how to squeeze two bedrooms and a full bathroom upstairs and clad the walls in clapboard. I kept the nonworking knob-and-tube wiring for nostalgia's sake and uncovered the good wooden floors hidden beneath decades of quick fixes. There would be no carpet for beach sand to rest in; I painted a trompe l'oeil runner on the stairs instead. And of course, cedar shingles replaced all of that siding.

My mom always said that if she could have named a cottage, she would have called it Back of the Moon, the fictitious name of an inn on an island in Maine in one of her favorite movies, *Leave Her to Heaven*, starring Gene Tierney. And so it is. I am so grateful that my mother could share my joy in having rescued an endangered species in this part of Maine. The last photo I have of her is of the two of us standing in the kitchen, the walls torn back to the studs. She passed away two weeks later, but her spirit lives on here, in this house, on this street, where I will always think of her and what she gave me: the extraordinary gift of Maine.

BACK OF

CAFÉ

ABOVE: Layers of linoleum had covered tidy wood floors, which I opted to leave raw. OPPOSITE: A painted runner gives beach sand little chance to hide on the stairs.

DREW
C R B

A HOUSE ON A WHARF

• • •

The Ping-Pong table in Polly Saltonstall's summer house has been the focus of some debate within the family for years. Should the ball land on the dead spot—worn from decades of fierce matches—point over. The more competitive members of the family find it galling. But to get a new table would be as strange as replacing the cast-iron stove in the kitchen with a stainless-steel Wolf.

For more than 130 years, the sprawling Saltonstall family has come home to the Fox Islands, taking up residence in various cottages, and gravitating in recent years to the nine-bedroom house on the harbor. "I came of age in this house," says Saltonstall, whose maternal grandmother acquired it in the 1940s, after it had been converted two decades earlier, one of a cluster of buildings on a commercial fishing wharf. "It looks pretty much the way it did when she was alive," she says.

Generations on, a reverence for family, history, and the future has mitigated any impulse to change much of anything at all. Indeed, to fiddle with the interior would be to tamper with its soul. It's hard to imagine her grandfather's flags—awards from yacht races that defined island summers then as they do now—festooned anywhere else but here, in a room overlooking the sea where he tacked and jibed his way to victory. Replace Grandmother's beloved wind-up Victrola with iTunes? "When

Granite pilings, raised two feet almost a decade ago to address rising tides, have sturdily supported the Saltonstall home for more than a century.

I first met my husband, I took him out to the house and played a record of bird calls on it," says Saltonstall. To swap out the serviceable sofa with a sectional would instantly give the place an identity crisis. Painted furniture and floors, country curtains, old framed photographs, pleated-print lampshades, and chintz cushions simply belong here.

"This island is frozen in time, in the best possible way," says Saltonstall. It is a sentiment she wants to pass on to the two teenage sons she shares with John Hanson. Together, she and Hanson publish *Maine Boats, Homes & Harbors* magazine. It's a tall order in the hyper-connected world the boys find themselves in. But Saltonstall insists that they spend a good part of the summer in the place their great-grandparents cherished so much. "My older son taught sailing one summer and it was a revelation," she says.

PRECEDING PAGES: Little has been rearranged inside, including Grandfather Saltonstall's photographs, despite their tilting this way and that.

ABOVE: Most of the cottage's nine bedrooms feature pairs of twin beds, all the better to accommodate a sprawling extended family.
OPPOSITE: Polly's mother painted the landscape over the bookcase.

Centennial
James A. Michener
James A. Michener
THE GLORY of the VIOLIN
THE YEAR OF THE FRENCH

ABOVE: No upgrades for this kitchen: pots and pans hang from nails driven into the wall, and the original cast-iron stove has pride of place. OPPOSITE: Bound copies of the British satire magazine *Punch* line a bookcase in the great room, where a cheetah print and floral chintzes genially coexist.

OVERLEAF: Many of the paintings in the house were made by islanders and purchased at the annual art show; a smattering hang on a guest bedroom wall.

A FISH HOUSE

• • •

It was swept away with the tide in the 1920s and rebuilt soon thereafter. But for as long as Bob Zuke can remember, the simple shingled shack used by commercial fishermen to maintain and repair their ropes, nets, and buoys was in a state of disrepair. As a young sternman in the 1970s and '80s, he motored past it daily, occasionally asking the owner if he might sell. Nope. In the 1990s, the building collapsed. Zuke persisted long after he traded in fishing for building, salvaging, and roofing. Almost twenty years later, the pile of rubble was his.

Zuke's family goes back three generations; his wife Linda's, four. Both were determined to restore the fish house for their sons—two of whom are commercial lobstermen—and future generations of Zukes. But for all of his looking toward the future, Zuke's heart is set firmly in the past. Indeed, this is a man who bought an ailing Victorian from the local historical society for one dollar, moved it four miles down the road, revived it, and filled it with treasures he has stored in a handful of barns in the area. "I want to be surrounded by as many antiques and old buildings as possible," he says.

To that end, he endeavored to use materials typical of century-old coastal properties and filtered it through inspiration taken from the Hardy Boys books he read as a kid. "They always seemed to be on the coast in some mystical and mysterious place. The lightning rods on the roof take me right back," says Zuke.

Clad in the same Atlantic white cedar shingles of the original, the house on stilts is built entirely with chemical-free materials, apart from the pressure-treated

Zuke salvaged the lightning rods that line the rooftop from an inn in a nearby town. "I was going for that Hardy Boys mystique," he says.

OPPOSITE: A simple rail recalls that of a ship and reminds visitors that water surrounds them. ABOVE: Zuke fitted out the kitchen with repurposed cabinets brightened by beadboard coated in its original green paint.

pilings required by the town. To outfit the inside, a plumbing- and electricity-free single room, Zuke dipped into the salvage stashed in his barns. Fir beadboard rescued from a cottage renovation on a nearby island lines the walls. A Portland-made Queen Atlantic cast-iron stove—once as ubiquitous in Maine kitchens as their stainless-steel replacements—is one of dozens Zuke has been gifted for the courtesy of hauling it away. A slate sink serves as a receptacle for water boiled on the stove; a bucket underneath is the catch-all. More than half a dozen oil lamps, their heights controlled by counterweights, are hung between hardy beams to illuminate the space.

It all could seem a tad slick for the fish business, and Zuke admits he has had to explain himself on occasion. "Time will take its toll, in the best possible way," he says. In the meantime, the Zukes might wade through the tidal marsh in their muck boots, climb the ladder, and enjoy a drink at sunset. But it will always be a place to carry on the lobstering tradition that defines this place. "The truth is, I wanted it to be so appealing that when people saw it, they would wish they were fishermen," says Zuke.

SANFORD

Queen
Atlantic

PRECEDING PAGES: A cast-iron Atlantic stove—Zuke has salvaged dozens—warms the fish house on chilly days.

OPPOSITE: Zuke raided his stash of oil lanterns and hung a dozen of them from the beams.

LEFT: He salvaged the old post office sign and found a perfect fit for it above a pair of windows.

BELOW: Life imitates art; the view out the windows flanks a pair of paintings depicting coastal Maine.

THE COTTAGES *at the* END OF THE ROAD

Carter Bedloe Smith's childhood reads like a fairy tale. He grew up on a Mid-Coast island largely forgotten in the off-season, where the main road dead-ends at the ocean. "I used to hide in the pines for so long that it would scare my parents," he says. The Smiths were three of the few hundred people, mostly lobstermen, who stuck it out in the winter. At seventeen and restless, Smith hopped on a bus to New York City, photography portfolio under his arm, and landed his first fashion magazine job. "It was the early 1990s and everyone was using artificial lights. I showed up with moody photos of girls in fields of flowers. All natural light," he says. An international career was born.

It wasn't long, though, before Smith realized that it didn't take ten-hour flights and five-star hotels to give him what he really needed. The answers were back on that dirt road to nowhere. One by one, Smith revived the four seaside cottages there that captivated him as a child so that folks from away could live the fairy tale too. His mission mirrored exactly the one

The porch at the Gills cottage, built in 1918, offers a front-row seat to the sunrise.

OPPOSITE: Smith stripped all of the sheetrock from Number 14, the tiniest cottage on the property, and left the studs exposed. ABOVE: The sunrise as seen through a cottage window on a chilly summer morning.

that won him his first magazine job all those years ago. "I'm always looking for the emotion in everything—a photo, a room, a landscape," he says.

To say that Smith's feelings have informed the antiques, furnishings, and *objets* collected from his far-flung travels is an understatement. An admitted compulsive shopper, he is more mad collector than connoisseur, using his gut as his guide. "I bought a four-and-a-half-foot clawfoot bathtub because I fell in love with it, put it in storage for twenty-four years, and found that it fit perfectly in Number 14, the one-room cottage," says Smith.

His is an analog world, where families gather undistracted but for the sound of the crashing waves and the sight of a regal osprey. There's nothing to do but cook, play Bananagrams, read—each place has a stack of Hardy Boy mysteries, a copy of *Jaws*, and books by E. B. White and Stephen King—and eat. "This is what I love the most about sharing these places. They give people a chance to experience Maine in a way that is completely disconnected from the crowds and the lines for lobster rolls."

EXPLORE HARPSWELL

THE DEAD ZONE
CUJO
CARRIE
THE TALISMAN
THE STAND
FROM A BUICK 8
NIGHTMARES & DREAMSCAPES
DANSE MACABRE
NIGHT SHIFT
CARRIE
THE DEAD ZONE
CHRISTINE
MISERY
PET SEMATARY
THE GIRL WHO LOVED TOM GORDON
ON WRITING
EYES OF THE DRAGON
DIFFERENT SEASONS
CHRISTINE
HEARTS IN ATLANTIS
FOUR PAST MIDNIGHT

PRECEDING PAGES: Smith suspended glass floats from the crystal chandelier in the open kitchen in Jacquish, the last cottage on the road before it meets the ocean.

OPPOSITE: Each cottage is stocked with a full complement of Hardy Boys, Nancy Drew, and Stephen King books.

CLOCKWISE FROM RIGHT: An adjacent barn is reflected in the window of the century-old Red House. Smith bought the 4½-foot-long bathtub more than two decades before he found a place for it in Number 14. A limited color palette holds together the fruits of Smith's scavenging: a painted chest of drawers, a Popsicle-stick lamp, a thrift shop painting, and velvet curtains.

OPPOSITE: Why not hang an anchor over the banister, itself adorned with antique wooden fish floats?
ABOVE: Smith purposely furnished a bedroom simply, so as not to distract from the view.

OVERLEAF: The Red House sits mere feet from the ocean, which pays the porch a visit at high tide.

HIGH HEAD

• • •

There is a set of drawers in the big bedroom at High Head that provides a glimpse into the disposition of the person who could dream up such a place. Painted words identify the contents of each drawer: shorts, super shorts, super-duper shorts, shirts, company shirts, good pants—no patches, patched pants, work sweaters, dressy ones, junk, and city junk.

One might not peg the owner as a professor of physics at MIT who directed the school's Weather Radar Research Project and worked on guided-missile technology during World War II. Such lofty achievements belied Alan Bemis's less serious side, the one that is on full display in this folly by the sea. "I just know that he and his wife wanted something fun and casual and not too stuffy," says his grandnephew John Maccone, who is the eighty-year-old property's conservator. "But I can't account for its unique styling," he says. Its name, on the other hand, reflects its siting—perched on a prominent rock easily visible to sailors.

Bemis's daughter Faith, who, together with her four sisters, spent every summer in the "kids' house," built separately from the stone

All of the materials used to build High Head came from the property, apart from the slate covering the roof, which was found in Vermont.

lighthouse that served as their parents' quarters, recalls her mother and father describing the summer cottage as Swedish. "But when they took us to Sweden as teenagers, we didn't see anything like it. Then we went to Norway and saw some places that looked a bit similar. So then we decided it was Norwegian," she says.

Whatever the inspiration, High Head, designed by Bemis and an architect friend and built in 1937 by fifty men using granite, spruce, fir, and white pine harvested on the property, remains largely the way Bemis would have liked it. The boom he installed in the sixty-foot-long living room to hang-dry the cotton sails from his beloved sloop, *Cirrus*, is still there, draped with an old sail Maccone found stashed on the property. Still, it can be a challenge to make updates without guilt. "I just don't want to disturb the going-back-in-time feeling," Faith says. "It's the one place my family can go to pretend that nothing bad is happening in the world."

ABOVE: Alan and Mary Bemis reserved the lighthouse for themselves; they slept and entertained there. OPPOSITE: The Bemises revived a defunct mill in New Hampshire to mill the spruce, fir, and pine trees felled on the property and used throughout.

BAR

ABOVE: An old cotton sail hung from the boom of Bemis's sloop, *Cirrus*, pays homage to him in the soaring great room. OPPOSITE: A brick parquet floor and granite walls, warmed by the sun, fit seamlessly into the rugged Maine landscape.

JUNK
CITY SHIRTS
WORK SHIRTS
COMPANY SHIRTS
GOOD PANTS - NO PATCHES
PATCHED-PANTS
WORK SWEATERS
CITY JUNK
TIES
SOCKS
DRAWERS
PAJAMAS
SHORTS
SUPER-SHORTS
SUPER-DUPER-SHORTS
FANCY-PANTS

MAINE

PAGE 76: Bemis didn't relegate the laundry room to a dark corner of the house but gave it a decorative flourish in the apex.

PAGE 77: Built-in drawers kept Bemis's clothes uniquely organized.

PRECEDING PAGES: High Head exudes a Nordic sensibility both inside and out.

ABOVE: Those seated at the table pushed up against the picture window are invited to look in just one direction—into the surrounding woods.

OPPOSITE: Little has changed in the kitchen, apart from a Formica countertop installed in the late 1970s.

FLOUR
SUGAR
COFFEE
TEA

REVERENCE
AND
RESTRAINT

A FARM BY THE SEA

Just twenty of the seventy saltwater farms that once rimmed this Mid-Coast island remain. And who knows what may have become of this one had the farmer who owned it until 1952 been able to purchase a pasteurizer. Instead, he sold the 1800s Cape to a couple of German psychoanalysts who found familiarity in the landscape: it felt like the Baltics. For the last thirty years, it has revealed itself to be fertile ground—figuratively and literally—for a retired couple who have largely lived in cities around the world. "We didn't think of it as a farm then. We just liked the view," says the wife.

And who could blame them? "I really wanted something out in the open, with lots of sky and room to really stretch out," she says. It didn't take long, however, before the pair realized that this land where cows once grazed had more going for it than an iconic view; it harbored some of the best soil on the island. To that end, they have begun to bring the farm back, working with a local vegetable farmer who will manage a chunk of their 140 acres.

For a cosmopolitan couple, it could read as folly or fairy tale. But this house and land have proven to be their center of gravity. "The older we get, the more we miss the countryside. And the more time we spend so close to nature, the more clearly we can see what is happening to the planet. We need to pay attention," says the wife.

In the early nineteenth century, it was easier to access an island home by the water; that's why the front door faces the sea.

Such awareness informed their decision to fiddle as little as possible with the house itself, inside and out. Filled with art, furniture and *objets* collected over years of living abroad, the rooms have the unmistakable air of a well-traveled life. But much of the action happens in the kitchen, a combination of the original summer and milking kitchens, where preparing and preserving the foods they grow has become a passion.

When viewed from the water, the scene is an Andrew Wyeth painting come to life. "We could have added dormers upstairs on the water side to get the views, but then that gloriously timeless view of the house from the fields and water would have been gone and that would have made us sad," says the wife. Instead, they sleep—soundly—under the eaves. "We've lived all over the world, but nothing compares to living here. I love its raffishness. It's the wild west, with lowercase w's."

ABOVE: A timelessness pervades the property, a place this peripatetic family calls its center of gravity. OPPOSITE: Painted floors and walls provide a neutral backdrop for the couple's eclectic collection of rugs and textiles.

OPPOSITE: A commemorative plate of Dwight and Mamie Eisenhower—a house gift—inspired a growing collection in the dining room, affectionately called the Presidential Room. José Martí, the father of Cuban independence, presides over it all.

CLOCKWISE FROM ABOVE LEFT: Art collected from around the world fills the house, including the original back stairway. Sleeping under the eaves is the tradeoff for maintaining the architectural integrity of the Cape. One of the two guest cabins that were originally rented to artists by the farmer who owned the property.

OVERLEAF: The kitchen was once two: a "modern" kitchen for domestic life and another with a cement floor for milk bottling.

MAS FINA

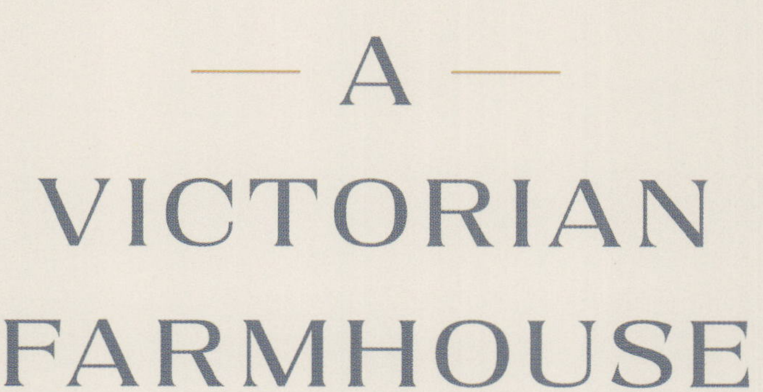

A VICTORIAN FARMHOUSE

California native Jordana Munk Martin's roots run deep in the low Sierras, where her cattle-ranching family has had an intimate relationship with the land for generations. So it may seem curious that the coast of Maine, with its lush landscape, dramatic granite ledges, and so much sea, cast its spell on her. "When I first visited here at nineteen, I just couldn't believe what I was looking at and decades later, I still can't believe what I am looking at," she says.

Which is exactly what her family said when Munk Martin and her husband, Ross, decided to buy a tumbledown Victorian on the Mid-Coast. But the pair found it easy to look straight past the *Stranger Things*–style addition and sunroom done up in 1970s ski lodge décor, and out to the meadow that led to the ocean and so much sky. "The blue outside the window changes every hour," says Munk Martin. And she is one to notice.

A love of sculptural objects inspired the couple to paint the house black; it becomes a shape in the landscape.

LEFT: An addition with numerous windows replaced one that was built in the 1970s.

OPPOSITE: A sculptural wood-burning stove is the centerpiece of the light-filled family room.

OVERLEAF: A collection of sentimental objects, both inherited and found, line the stairway wall, painted in Farrow & Ball's Stiffkey Blue.

The color blue has become synonymous with Munk Martin, a textile artist and founder of Brooklyn-based Tatter, an organization that explores the role of cloth in culture, and its attendant library, Blue, home to thousands of volumes and objects related to textiles. She comes by her love of the color honestly, if not genetically. Her grandmother, the fine artist Edith Wyle, founded the Los Angeles Craft & Folk Art Museum (now Craft Contemporary) and began collecting Japanese textiles in the early 1960s. Munk Martin's mother, a ceramicist, was equally passionate about them. When both passed away, she inherited the textiles, most dyed with indigo. "I unpacked my mother's house and her mother's house into the Maine house," she says of the decidedly non-period interiors.

"But that's the thing about Maine. It appeals to your creative side, your wilder side, your frontier side. It makes you want to homestead. It makes you want to be off the grid. And there's anarchy in that. And so there is something anarchic about overriding the vernacular of this house and doing our own thing. That is what I relate to when I am in Maine."

OPPOSITE: A pine chest of drawers warms a corner of the guest room. ABOVE: The stair landing is roomy enough to accommodate a daybed fitted with a ticking mattress.

OVERLEAF: A patchwork French quilt, purchased from the Marston House (see pages 262–69) hangs on the floating wall that separates the bedroom from the bath.

ABOVE: Munk Martin convinced Sharon Mrozinski of the Marston House to sell the display piece that now holds her collection of ceramics.

LEFT: Munk Martin also displays her ceramics collection in a cabinet from India. The painting on the back wall is by friend and artist Bayard Hollins.

OPPOSITE: The kitchen floor tiles are a favorite Japanese pattern called Asano-ha.

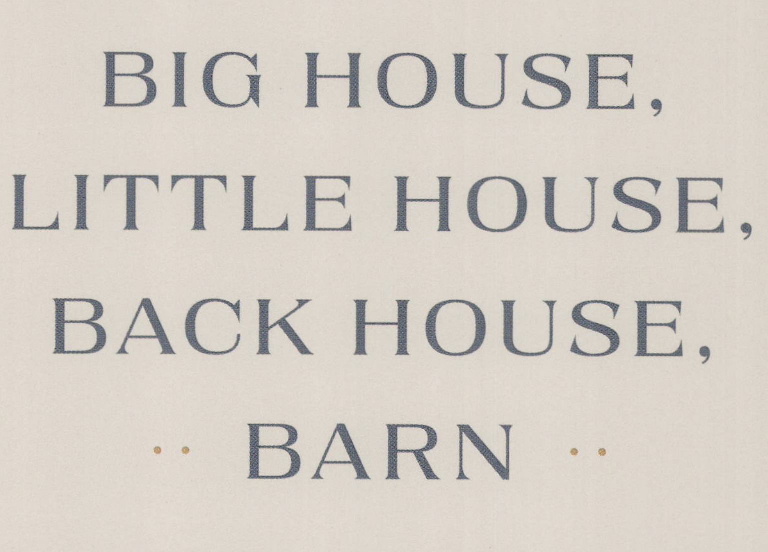

BIG HOUSE, LITTLE HOUSE, BACK HOUSE, BARN

Connected farm buildings began to appear all over rural New England in the nineteenth century, not, as is commonly believed, for protection on the trek from big house to barn during the region's frigid winters. The arrangements grew out of Yankee practicality, set up for the mix of industry that took place there: growing crops, raising animals, and making crafts and clothing.

How fitting, then, that photographer and lighting designer Chris Baker and his wife, Odette Heideman, a literary editor and ceramicist, fell for an 1850s Cape and its attachments while visiting a friend Down East several summers ago. Not that tending crops and cows was part of the plan, but producing and creating has long been in their DNA.

"Our goal is to make as many of the things that we live with as possible," says Baker, whose delicate curtain rods, light fixtures, and built-in shelving provide the armature for handmade linens and Heideman's pottery collections. Every room, each one dedicated to a single purpose—eating, reading, sleeping—is a reflection of the couple's aim. A sophisticated mix of paintings and photographs, textiles, lighting, and objects mingle with modern and antique

The kitchen occupies the little-house portion of the Baker property.

ABOVE: Baker stacked four cords of wood chopped from a felled tree on the property Scandinavian-style, in a beehive shape. OPPOSITE: The bookcase of unfinished marine-grade plywood holds a mix of collected ceramics as well as Heideman's creations.

furnishings, tricking even the most astute into thinking that the couple, parents to two grown daughters, have lived in this place forever.

This is the home of artists who see creative possibility and utility everywhere. For Baker, who studied botany, the seven-acre field behind the house provides endless natural curiosities that have become the subject of his photographs. Dying maple and pine trees yielded firewood that he stacked Scandinavian-style into a sculptural beehive. Heideman has searched out Maine granite chips to incorporate into the Japanese-style clays she uses, and she mixes granite dust into her glazes, some made from the pine and maple ash on their land. Morning walks yield seaweed that she boils to make funori, a gel-like substance used to render slips more brushable. They've even planted red-stemmed willow from which to make teapot handles.

Their surroundings have provided the pair with much, but both Baker and Heideman agree that it is the big house, little house, back house, and especially the barn as work space that brought them to this place, far more remote—and expansive—than their prior home on Long Island's East End. Says Baker, "Moving into this home gave us not only the space but the permission to do what we really want to do. Everything else is the cream on top."

OPPOSITE: White paint—high gloss, eggshell, and flat—visually expands the light-filled rooms. ABOVE: A painting by Lulu Miller, Heideman's sister, hangs over the entry to the kitchen.

OPPOSITE AND ABOVE: In the big house, the dining room features a timelessly appealing mix of antique, vintage, and modern pieces. A tiny oil painting, a sketch for a larger work, is framed perfectly by a secret door.

OPPOSITE: The barn doubles as guest quarters and a breezy space for summer dinner parties.

ABOVE: Heideman's childhood bed fills the sleeping loft.

LEFT: Who needs a bookcase when a ball of twine will do?

OPPOSITE: Pieces in the OH pottery line await firing.
ABOVE: A misty morning view from Heideman's studio.

A MINI MODERNIST COMPOUND

When Nadja Zerunian and Nick van Praag were expats living in Washington, D.C., they spent weekends looking at beach houses in the area. "We were intrigued by this American idea of indoor-outdoor living that seemed so typical of East Coast summers," says Zerunian, who is Austrian. Each time they were set to make an offer, van Praag, who is British, would back out. "He had this Maine fantasy," she says. Their first visit was anything but.

An island stay over a freezing, rainy week in June left Zerunian with a miserable cold. "I wondered who was crazy enough to vacation in such a place," she says. A friend insisted they persevere, and provided a twenty-four-hour tour of restaurants, concerts, films, and beaches on the mainland. "It was so overwhelming, we couldn't wait to get back to the island," says Zerunian.

It wasn't the summer house they had imagined, but the tiny wreck of a place, built in the early 1970s, was compelling, not least because the views are stunning. "The enormity of the pines and the sky dwarfed it so much that it barely registers in the landscape," says Zerunian.

As the couple embarked on rehabilitating the 800-square-foot house—three connected structures resembling classic Maine boathouses—they noticed that every measure was a multiple of four, suggesting that it was a rigorously principled design. Only later did they learn that the builder studied under Walter

Simple structures were designed to blend seamlessly into the landscape, as if sprung from the granite outcroppings they are built on.

Gropius at Harvard. "Here we were, dreaming of the perfect American house and we wind up with one by a disciple of the Bauhaus," says Zerunian.

Several years in, they asked Harvard-trained local architect Riley Pratt to design a trio of freestanding cottages connected by decks for their three grown children; together they mimic a disassembled version of the main house. Inspired by an Alvar Aalto design, two are devoted to sleeping and one is designed for communal cooking and relaxing. "We couldn't get away from our European roots," says Zerunian.

But they get away. The couple, whose NGO work takes them from their Vienna home to chaotic places around the globe, have found what Zerunian describes as their "dreamy place at the end of the world." From June to September, they feel such a profound connection to nature that the return to urban life is trying. "When you live in cities, your life goes on no matter what the sky is doing, but when you live in a place like Maine, especially on an island, everything depends on the weather."

OPPOSITE: Standing-seam roofs and cross-laminated timber clad the trio of connected cottages.
ABOVE: The kitchen in the communal cottage is sparse. "You realize just how little you need," says Zerunian.

OVERLEAF LEFT: A ladder designed for picking apples leads to a loft space over the library.
OVERLEAF RIGHT: The couple chose furnishings that honor the modernist ethos of the compound.

FEMALE
CHAMPION

OPPOSITE: The structures read Scandinavian, but the landscape is unmistakably Maine.

CLOCKWISE FROM ABOVE LEFT: A self-described lapsed minimalist, Zerunian's collections, including an artfully hung group of daguerreotypes, are scattered about the property. Nature makes for the best décor. The American-made fireplace, based on a French 1960s design, swivels.

GEORGE E.

AN ANTIQUE CAPE

• • •

If it were up to Bess Piergrossi, she would never leave the rural property in southern Maine she shares with her husband, Michael, a chef. "The feeling is inexplicable. It is as if there is some kind of magnetic force here that proffers happiness and safety," she says.

Or maybe it's the cows in the barn. Piergrossi had long nursed a fantasy to work on a dairy farm, so the couple, who were then living on the coast, abandoned Maine for the verdant pastures of Vermont. "I got my wish there, but it was very difficult to make a living," says Piergrossi. The experience did clarify a few things, namely, how the pair really wanted to live. They headed back to Maine, this time inland, where the 1740s Cape they live in practically fell in their lap. And it just happened to be the original homestead on a working dairy farm, where Piergrossi milks cows three days each week.

Only four families have inhabited the clapboard and shingle house, its previous owner doing it up in cliché colonial decor: painted floors, historic colors, period furniture. The Piergrossis stripped it raw to reveal the natural beauty of the hulking ceiling beams, plaster

A graveyard on the property traces back seven generations—more than 200 years—to the original owners of the house.

ABOVE: The Piergrossis stripped the interior raw, left the floors and the beams that way, and painted the walls the purest white. OPPOSITE: Open shelves in the kitchen express the home's aesthetic: simple beauty.

walls, and pine floors, then filled it with simple, functional furniture. A pair of planks set on a base found in an antiques shop serves as a dining table. Piergrossi repurposed a piece of farming equipment she found in the barn to hold a stack of wood. She made use of nails driven into a kitchen ceiling beam by hanging pots from them. A nor'easter lamp serves as a talisman; the couple bought it when they first moved to Maine.

A sense of calm pervades the Piergrossi home, but it belies a Yankee industriousness that finds the pair presiding over chickens, ducks, and yes, cows. There is a vegetable and flower garden, too, and a seasonal flower stand on the side of the nearby road. "I keep thinking about ways I can make a living from this land," says Piergrossi. And who could blame her? The commute to the barn, or church, as Piergrossai calls it, is a hundred-foot walk.

For now, however, the couple is happy to take it one day at a time. "Our house really helped solidify for us our position in the world, in our town. It's our haven. I think a lot of times when people think of Maine they think of coast and water, but that is not our experience of Maine; ours is land based."

French-American Cooking
oman's World Cook Book ~ Wallace
MASTERING CHEESE
THE ANARCHIST COOKBOOK

ABOVE: The couple sought to honor the bones of the house by exposing them—and left the imperfections to celebrate its legacy. OPPOSITE: A neighbor cut the two planks that sit on the dining table base, an antiques shop find.

OPPOSITE: Whereas some might have opted to add a dormer to make for more headroom in the bedroom, the Piergrossis deferred to the Cape's original design. ABOVE: All of the furniture in the house is passed down, found, or repurposed, and it all seamlessly suits the spaces.

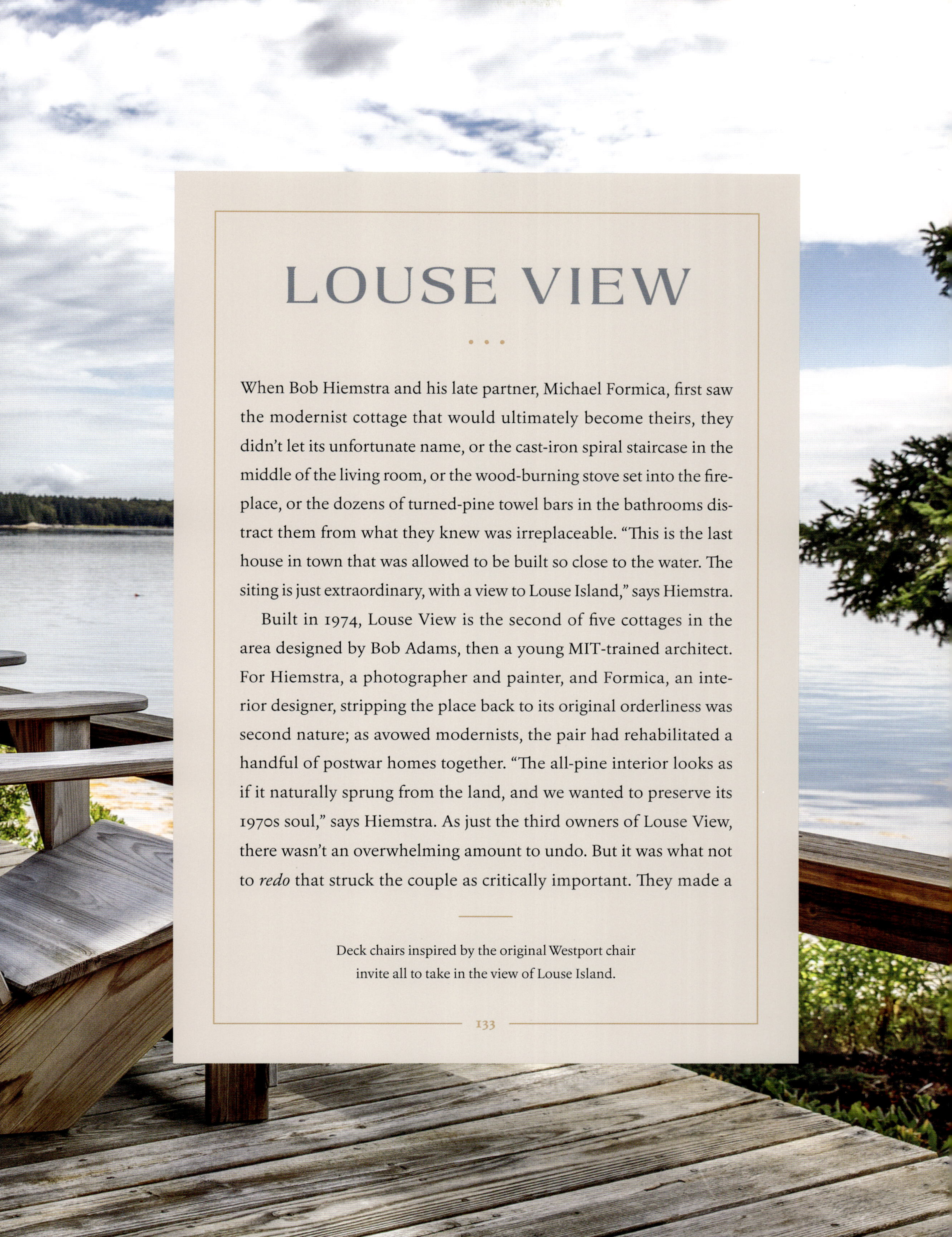

LOUSE VIEW

When Bob Hiemstra and his late partner, Michael Formica, first saw the modernist cottage that would ultimately become theirs, they didn't let its unfortunate name, or the cast-iron spiral staircase in the middle of the living room, or the wood-burning stove set into the fireplace, or the dozens of turned-pine towel bars in the bathrooms distract them from what they knew was irreplaceable. "This is the last house in town that was allowed to be built so close to the water. The siting is just extraordinary, with a view to Louse Island," says Hiemstra.

Built in 1974, Louse View is the second of five cottages in the area designed by Bob Adams, then a young MIT-trained architect. For Hiemstra, a photographer and painter, and Formica, an interior designer, stripping the place back to its original orderliness was second nature; as avowed modernists, the pair had rehabilitated a handful of postwar homes together. "The all-pine interior looks as if it naturally sprung from the land, and we wanted to preserve its 1970s soul," says Hiemstra. As just the third owners of Louse View, there wasn't an overwhelming amount to undo. But it was what not to *redo* that struck the couple as critically important. They made a

Deck chairs inspired by the original Westport chair invite all to take in the view of Louse Island.

conscious choice to keep the linoleum floors in the bathroom and the Formica countertops in the kitchen. Both felt that if they replaced them with marble and tile, the rest of the place would look pretty bleak.

Filled with art and *objets* collected over many years, it would seem that Hiemstra and Formica had Louse View in mind long before they purchased it in 2017. "We bought pieces that resonated with us, which means that they generally work together. But we also made a conscious effort to collect Maine art since we started coming here decades ago," says Hiemstra.

Indeed, the couple never had any impulse to introduce luxuries they might enjoy elsewhere. "Michael liked to call it our version of sleep-away camp," says Himestra. The lure is the drama in the sky and sea. "He always marveled at the uniquely starlit skies. And the drama! We once watched a bald eagle pick a seagull out of the air right in front of the house. Where else would you see that?"

ABOVE: An outsize drawing of the common American chigger, one of three the couple had purchased three decades ago, found a home in Maine.
OPPOSITE: A sofa upholstered in Letters by Danish designer Gunnar Aagaard Andersen sits beneath a collection—much of it by Maine artists—that spans three decades.

OVERLEAF: The view to Louse Island from the deep-water dock.

ABOVE: A bust of John Muir presides over the entryway. OPPOSITE: Though the house featured "pine for days," there was no temptation to whitewash it; Hiemstra and Formica consciously kept the space's envelope in the 1970s.

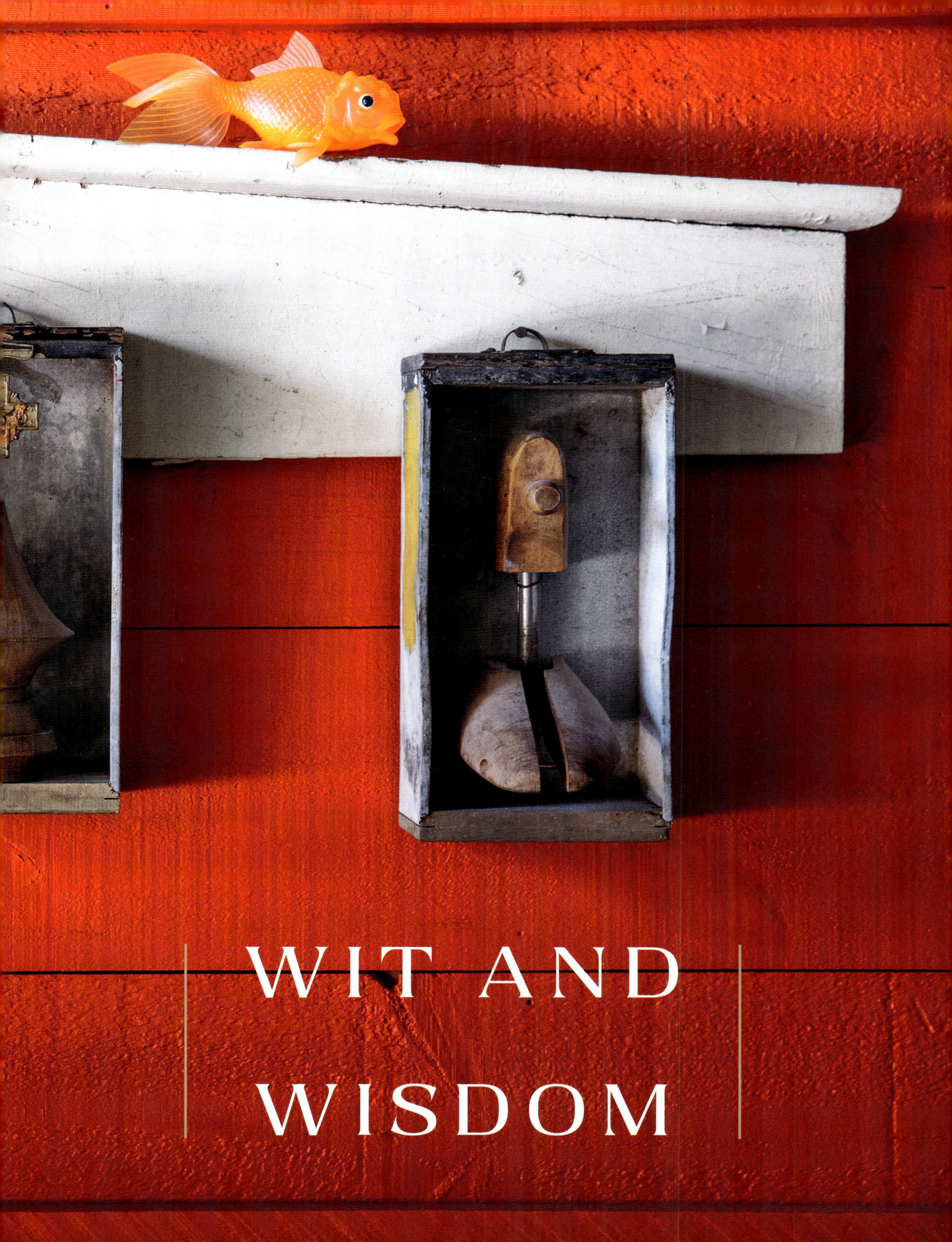

WIT AND WISDOM

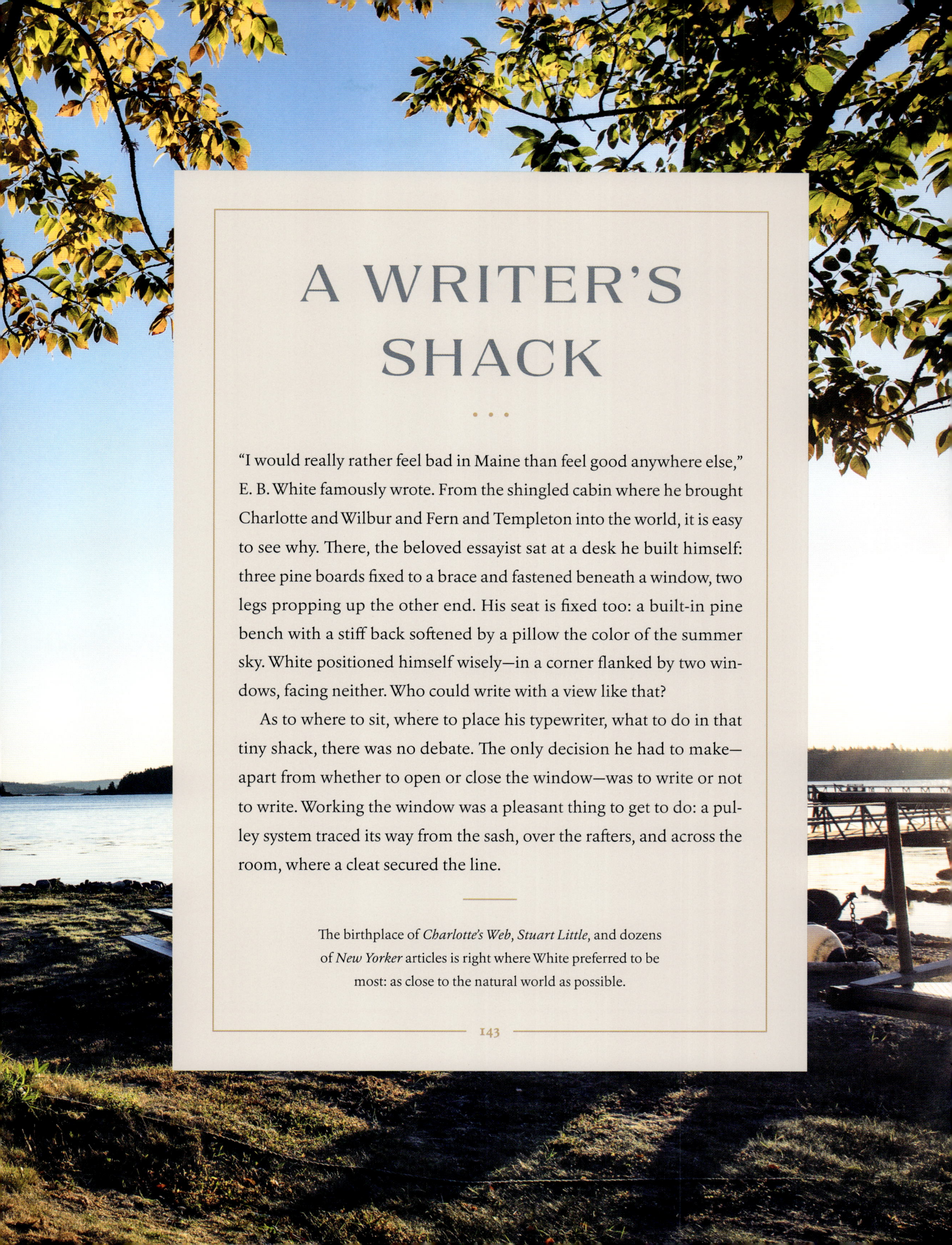

A WRITER'S SHACK

"I would really rather feel bad in Maine than feel good anywhere else," E. B. White famously wrote. From the shingled cabin where he brought Charlotte and Wilbur and Fern and Templeton into the world, it is easy to see why. There, the beloved essayist sat at a desk he built himself: three pine boards fixed to a brace and fastened beneath a window, two legs propping up the other end. His seat is fixed too: a built-in pine bench with a stiff back softened by a pillow the color of the summer sky. White positioned himself wisely—in a corner flanked by two windows, facing neither. Who could write with a view like that?

As to where to sit, where to place his typewriter, what to do in that tiny shack, there was no debate. The only decision he had to make—apart from whether to open or close the window—was to write or not to write. Working the window was a pleasant thing to get to do: a pulley system traced its way from the sash, over the rafters, and across the room, where a cleat secured the line.

The birthplace of *Charlotte's Web*, *Stuart Little*, and dozens of *New Yorker* articles is right where White preferred to be most: as close to the natural world as possible.

OPPOSITE: White's humor is reflected in the single document tacked to the wall: the Newsbreak Department Heads at the *New Yorker*.

LEFT: White tied a dinghy anchor to the end of the rope that he used to open and close the picture window facing the sea.

Each morning, White walked from the house, attached to the great shingled barn where Charlotte and friends lived, along the path set off by a pair of split-rail fences, to his writing shack. His caretaker, Henry Allen, walked beside him, carrying his Underwood portable typewriter. At the end of the day, they did the walk in reverse. White and Allen walked back and forth together every day.

White's work for the *New Yorker* sometimes required his presence in the magazine's Manhattan offices. On one occasion, during the writing of *Charlotte's Web*, he was particularly furious to get the call. A stickler for accuracy, he had been studying the behavior of a particular spider in the barn. It had spun an egg sac the day before White was set to travel, so he brought it with him and kept it in a ventilated box in his city apartment. In the following weeks, baby spiders were festooned about the house, to his housekeeper's dismay and his great delight.

A storied career, a loving family, strong friendships—White enjoyed them all. But his love of the natural world and its inhabitants stood apart. In his inimitable style, White summed it up tidily, "All that I hope to say in books, all that I ever hope to say, is that I love the world."

OPPOSITE: The dock stretches out beyond the shallow water, far enough into the deep to allow boats to be tied up.

•

CLOCKWISE FROM ABOVE LEFT: White kept essentials for Maine living nearby: a good beach chair, a life preserver, and a fishing net. Yankee thrift dictates that windows are necessary only where the views are. A wood-burning stove insured that cold weather could not interrupt White's writing routine.

•

OVERLEAF: The barn where Charlotte was born is connected to the big house by a back house.

ART HOUSE

• • •

"I didn't mean to install my art all over the house," says Lauren Gillette. She didn't really mean to live in Maine either. But a year-long experiment on the southern coast with her husband and young daughter converted the former Bostonians forever. "The truth is, I wasn't convinced after that first year. I was dragging a heater from room to room all winter," says Gillette. As time went on, however, the visual artist realized that the parts of city life that eluded her—time and freedom to make work—were in abundance here.

And does she ever make work. Twenty-five years later, Gillette's practice is writ large in the house that serves as both studio and family home. The "contractor's special," as its owner refers to the humble cottage she inherited from her father, was typical of the single-story summer houses once ubiquitous in this part of southern Maine, set one street back from the beach. Over the years, it gained two stories, one fully devoted to Gillette's studio, though life and work appear to spill over into each other.

In every room, the words are flying. Paintings, too, animate the spaces. "I really can't help myself. No surface is sacred," says Gillette. Here, a portrait painted on a headboard leans against the built-in bookcases, while two other portraits are propped up on her desk. There, a quote from *Peyton Place* (filmed in Mid-Coast Maine) covers the backrest of a chair, while

Not surprisingly, Gillette left no surface uncovered in the living room, where she painted her mother to greet all who made their way up the stairs. Her daughter glued all the shells onto the drop-leaf desk.

T-BONE.
2 beef shins
small amount teriyaki sauce
small amount Worcestershire
2 c. chopped celery
Indian summer is like a
Ripe, hotly passionate,
fickle,she comes and go
she pleases so that one
never sure whether she w
come at all, nor for how lo
she will stay.
Grace Metaliou
STEPHANIE KALLOS
Sing Them Home
CON THIEN
THE HILL OF ANGELS

ABOVE: A reclining nude, painted on a headboard picked up at a yard sale, was inspired by Polish portrait painter Tamara de Lempicka. OPPOSITE: Inspiration is everywhere; on a closet door, quotes and images include a profile of the irrepressible Diana Vreeland.

more words shout out from pillows. Almost any surface is fair game for the artist's verbal visuals. Leather jackets are armatures for historical thought, jeans are the canvas for lyrics to a favorite song, and an overflow of food quotes covers the kitchen chalkboard. She papered the bathroom walls with the rejection letter from a prominent publishing house.

The prolific artist points to her folk singer mother for instilling in her a love of words and to her education—the curriculum was grounded in the Bauhaus principle of learning how to learn—for wanting to teach herself something new with every project. "I have the impulse to use whatever is in front of me to make my art. If I was in jail, I would make soap dolls," she says.

In that unlikely event, Gillette would surely miss the place that once gave her pause. "I still think of myself as a Massachusetts girl, but I love Maine. The beach! It's like the circus. It gets into your blood. I walk it every single morning, no matter the season, no matter the weather."

HOLLYWOOD BABYLON
What I Saw and How I Lied
KEN FOLLETT
THE KEY TO REBECCA
BARACK OBAMA
Dreams from My Father
American
Cesar's Way
CESAR MILLAN
HOW TO BUILD A GIRL
Georgia O'Keeffe
GEORGIA O'KEEFFE A PORTRAIT BY ALFRED STIEGLITZ
ANNIE LEIBOVITZ WOMEN SUSAN SONTAG
Irving Penn
10 YEARS OF DOLCE & GABBANA
ERIC FISCHL
EAT IT OR WEAR IT LAUREN GILLETTE
EAT IT OR WEAR IT LAUREN GILLETTE
EAT IT OR WEAR IT LAUREN GILLETTE
EAT IT OR WEAR IT LAUREN GILLETTE
BARSON
HELLER
Sterling
California
LACMA
UNIVERSE
ARCHITECTURE
UNIVERSE
FRANK LLOYD WRIGHT IN POP-UP
Iain Thomson
Character Is Destiny
John McCain
The Negative
Adams
HOLLYWOOD GAYS
Oxford
Literary Terms
LEE CHILD
Night School
Hollywood:
LET'S BRING BACK
THE LAZLO LETTERS By DON NOVELLO
THE MYSTERIES OF HARRIS BURDICK
THE SECRET KNOWLEDGE OF GROWN-UPS
CLEOPATRA'S NOSE
ITALIAN STYLE
HOW TO MAKE MODERN JEWELRY
MARGARET BOURKE-WHITE
SURFING
MEXICANA
I CAN MAKE YOU SLEEP
Where the Sidewalk Ends

OPPOSITE: A belly-dancing bra, brought back from Egypt by a friend, hangs from the shelf where Gillette keeps her sketchbooks.

RIGHT: Why not mount a rococo gold frame onto a chalkboard—and then use it to frame a favorite adage?

BELOW: In Gillette's top-floor studio, she surrounds herself with reminders of her former life as a portrait painter. She clad the cheap paneled walls in copper, then painted two coats of acid wash on them to achieve a patina.

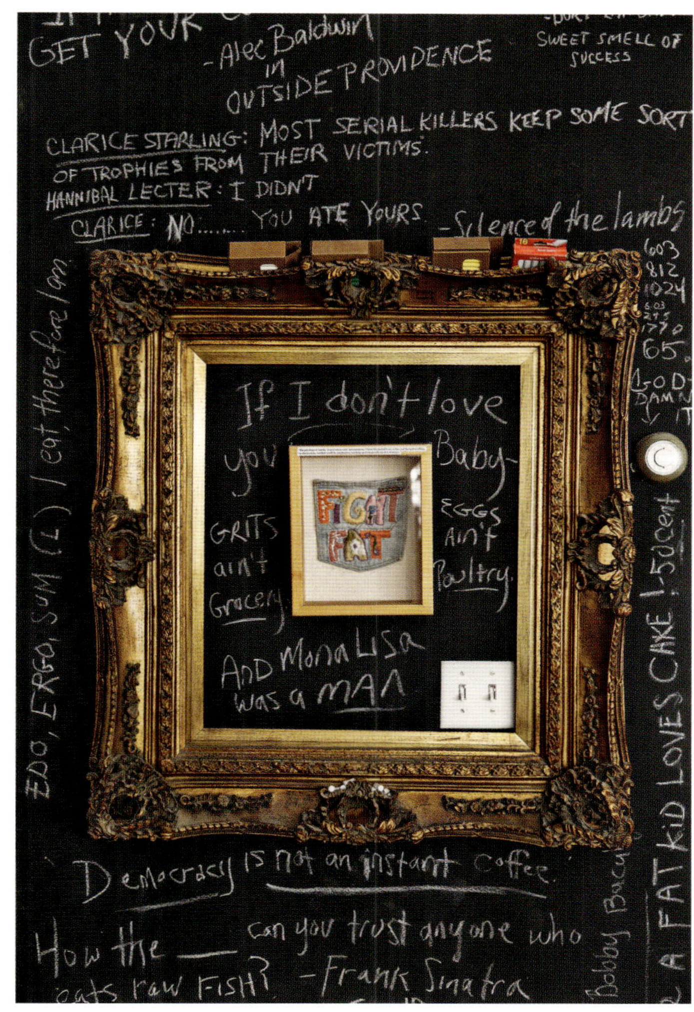

Kathleen Hackett

RED COTTAGE

• • •

We called it the silk purse project, because it started life as a sow's ear. The tiny, single-story camp, built in 1950 and abandoned for years, didn't have much going for it. But once inside, it was clear why its owners clung to the place for almost a half century. The idyllic pond. The majestic mountain. The gloating bullfrogs. The loon calls. The old-school floating dock just begging for a game of jump or dive. How could anyone let that go?

We had a secret weapon in the family; design/build team Tom Young and his wife, my sister Mary Ann, who live in the village nearby, did what they do best—transform rather than tear down. In just a few months, Red Cottage, named for the color of its trim and new roof shingles, grew a polite story taller and wore a classic coat of cedar shingles to blend into the surrounding pines and birches.

For almost two decades, my husband, Stephen, and I, and our sons, Finn and James, made our ritual summer exodus from the city. The late June, eight-hour drive to Maine inevitably became twelve because there was a cabin to furnish, and there was no better resource than the flea markets, antiques cooperatives, and tag sales so ubiquitous along the coast.

A summer cottage is not a summer cottage unless there is a screen door, typically one in need of a little repair.

OPPOSITE: Humor is a family trait, as evinced in the homage paid to the biggest fish we ever caught, hanging over a thrift-shop painting of nearby Mt. Battie.

RIGHT: Framed leaves picked up on our travels line the bathroom walls from floor to ceiling.

OVERLEAF: Drinking straws made for an excellent rainy-day project; the sculpture that hangs from the ceiling grew every year.

We invariably arrived under an ink-black sky sprayed with stars. The crickets, loons, and bullfrogs owned the night. In the early years, I would steal a swim across the pond while the babies slept, all that fresh air guaranteeing they would not awaken until I returned to our dock. When the boys were old enough to swim, Stephen created an underwater world of treasures, including a sunken model of the *Titanic*, china tea sets, and a jar of coins.

As if overnight, our toddlers turned into teenagers whose mere presence in the cottage shrunk it by half. We had squeezed every second of joy out of that 950 square feet; it was time to trade it in for a slightly larger model in a nearby village. It took just one day to pack up; we left most of the furniture behind and took only the sentimental things. The library of Hardy Boys, the tiny pairs of Keds, the rope sconces from Paris, the framed leaves from our travels.

As the screen door slammed one last time behind us, I caught a glimpse of the door jamb, where we had marked the boys' growth since they were old enough to stand. As my eyes filled up, Stephen prised it from the wall, carried it down to the car, and strapped it to the roof.

GO
FISH
LALANNE
DOISNEAU

ABOVE: A yellow-painted floor tinged the sun-flooded "back room," once a windowless storage room, with golden light.
OPPOSITE: Treasures from land and sea.

a few days in maine
august 2008

A HOUSE IN THE TREES

• • •

Most artists are drawn to Maine for the light, land, and sea. But for Dan Dowd, it was the proximity to a transfer station. "There are really great piles of wood and metal and so much more that is free for the taking," says the Massachusetts native. The castoffs rekindled an attraction to assemblage art, a practice that wasn't getting much of his attention while working for "the man" in Boston well into his thirties.

Dowd moved to Maine to change that. It was a high school art class where the seeds were first planted; his teacher spent summers on the coast and kept a pile of Down East magazines in the classroom. "I used to look at the real estate section and dream," he says. The fixer-upper he bought may not have made it into those pages—it was on the market for four years—but Dowd recognized that the benign '70s box merely suffered from an identity crisis. "It didn't really know what it was supposed to be," he says.

But he did. With a studio on the ground floor and living space above, here was a chance to make his largest assemblage yet. Overflowing with found—and bequeathed—objects most consider useless, Dowd has created a house-sized cabinet of curiosities. This is an artist who sees the sculptural in a steel spring, the humor in a plaster bust sporting a hat and sunglasses, and the possibility

Dowd painted the living room walls lobster red and the ceiling a dark gray. "From the outside, it looks like there is a fire going all of the time."

in a link of bicycle chain. “My work is about patina and history and time, which is so easy to find anywhere you go in Maine,” he says.

Notably, there’s not a shell, rock, or piece of driftwood to be seen. Apart from the lobster-red living room, lined from floor to ceiling with artwork collected since Dowd was a teen, there’s not a hint of clichéd coastal beauty here. “I’m really drawn to another kind of beauty, call it ugly beauty,” he says. One afternoon on a drive, he noticed that a handsome house he had long admired for its lack of paint was getting a new coat. As if by reflex, he pulled over and asked for one of the worn boards. “That piece of wood is a record of time, a connection to the past. That’s the thing about Maine. It makes you feel like you are connected to the planet.”

OPPOSITE: The more styles you mix, the better they go together; eye-popping Eames chairs surround an early 1900s drop-leaf walnut table in the dining room. ABOVE: The Empire buffet was the first piece of furniture Dowd ever bought. A coiled spring from a junkyard and a giant hanging hinge from a sliding barn door rest on top.

OVERLEAF: Works by artist friends fill the living room, as does the sound of the accordion, which Dowd began to play a decade ago.

PAGES 170–71: Dowd’s rubber sculptures mix with collected works in the studio on the ground floor.

Winslow Homer and the Camera
2008 BIENNIAL EXHIBITION
New York COOL Painting and Sculpture from the NYU Art Collection
WHY DRAW? 500 YEARS OF DRAWINGS AND WATERCOLORS
SARGENT to BASQUIAT
FLEMING
HANDCRAFTED MAINE
THE TULSE LUPER SUITCASES
CHUCK CLOSE
ANSELM KIEFER
PAST
FUTURES

William Wegman
Hello Nature
Bowdoin
FLAG & BANNER
Please Do Not Touch the Art
Children Must Be Supervised
EXCELSIOR

AN ARTIST'S RETREAT

• • •

Lois Dodd made one of her most notable bodies of work during the Watergate hearings in 1974. "I was painting in the woods near my house and ran back and forth to listen to the radio. It was like having office hours," she says. For more than half a century, the realist painter has found the land surrounding her Mid-Coast Maine farmhouse to be as fertile and endlessly exciting a subject as any. "I paint what I am looking at," says the plainspoken nonagenarian, who was part of the wave of postwar New York artists—her former husband, Bill King, and Alex Katz among them—to explore the coast of Maine in the 1950s. "The real estate was so cheap compared to Long Island, so we thought, why not?" she says.

Such pragmatism and fearlessness are on full display in the cedar-shingled house and barn where she has settled in for summers since 1964. It would be easy to assume that Dodd frames up all the action outdoors, as evinced by her paintings of window frames, sides of clapboard houses, woodland paths, geometric flowers, and laundry blowing in the breeze. But a decade after making those paintings of the woods, she mixed up some powdered pigment left over from her days as a student at Cooper Union and set to work on the walls in the north corner of the house.

One of Dodd's grandchildren installed a solar panel on the roof of the garden shed.

ABOVE: Dodd sits in her kitchen, framed by a four-paned window, many of which show up in her work. OPPOSITE: Works by friends hang in the dining room, an addition to the original farmhouse, in which the clapboard wall was once the exterior of the house.

"It was cold in that room until I tore down the kitchen wall and put in a stove. Then I decided it needed another window and some woods. *That* was fun," she says. Concerned the linoleum that once lined the kitchen floor would create rot underneath, she ripped it up and was left with black splotches from the glue holding it down. "I thought, I'll just do this spray-painty thing on it," she says. The most recent addition came in the form of red nail polish, applied by a houseguest.

In Dodd's studio, an early nineteenth-century New England barn, there are dozens of paintings neatly lining the whitewashed walls and piles of palettes hanging from nails. A flat file heaves with drawings. Her easel sits in the middle of the room, notably unencumbered—all the easier to extricate herself and get out into the surrounding woods and fields. "Being in Maine is what got me working outdoors," she says. "And for a time, I thought I would exhaust the subject and have to make a move. But that never happened."

Matisse
Alex Katz
WHY DRAW?
LANDSCAPE PAINTING NOW
COASTING
AMERICAN MODERN
MAINE GEOGRAPHIC
Wildlife Signatures
THE STORY OF LIGHTHOUSES
A FIELD GUIDE TO WILDFLOWERS

OPPOSITE: An adjacent dining room wall, clad in worn painted shingles, also once the exterior of the house. ABOVE: An imperfect floor inspired Dodd to mask it with paint that she sprayed and dripped indiscriminately.

LEFT: The artist's studio is ten steps from the house in a detached barn, where the only company is an occasional honeybee and a radio.

OPPOSITE: Nothing fancy here: Dodd sets the stage for her subjects using household objects.

RIGHT: Dodd surrounds herself with art everywhere; on walls, shelves, desks, and bureaus.

Klean-Strip

THE CIVIL WAR

OPPOSITE: Works by artist friends, among them Nancy Wissemann-Widrig, Jeff Epstein, and Barbara Sullivan, line a living room wall. ABOVE: Dodd painted over an earlier wall treatment in the sunny yellow that shows up throughout the cottage.

OVERLEAF: Every day is sunny in a once chilly ground-floor bedroom, where Dodd brought the outside in and painted the floor caution yellow.

WEATHERED
AND FREE

A COTTAGE ON A COVE

• • •

It takes guts to build a house from the ground up. It takes even more confidence to ask an artist to execute the plans in your absence. "We corresponded by snail mail, but I think there was one phone call about a bathtub," says the owner, whose ties Down East date to the early 1900s. In painter and sculptor Chris Baker, she and her husband found a kindred spirit. After all, this is a man who, at eighteen years old, threw the sheets off his eighteen-foot sailboat and set sail for Maine from his childhood home on the Connecticut coast. Decades and many moves later, he has found a way to get back here every year. For one of them, he made what his clients consider one of his most impressive works of art.

The mandate was straightforward. "We really just wanted a place to drop our stuff and get outside with our three children," says the wife, who, as the director of a summer camp in her early twenties, hired her future husband to assist her on wilderness trips.

The open-construction design, in which the frame is exposed on the interior, gave Baker the opportunity to take an artistic approach. Subtle

White cedar shingles weather to a desirable silvery patina with constant exposure to sun, salt, and rain.

LEFT: Baker specified locally milled spruce for the interior; each board was shiplapped, or shaped to fit snugly into the next.

OPPOSITE: Who needs cabinets when open construction provides shelves for you?

choices—using locally milled spruce, changing the dimensions of the rafters and studs by a quarter inch, squaring off the ends, and spacing them wider apart—might seem hair-splitting, but they are the deceptive details that give the interior a fighting chance for attention from this family of outdoor lovers. Baker was just as meticulous with the exterior, using white cedar shingles, western red cedar for the trim, and aluminum-framed windows to protect against the salt air; the place will never need a paint job.

It all suits this no-nonsense family to a T. The thirty-inch electric stove, Formica countertop, and mismatched furniture handed down from a grandfather who lived nearby are beloved for their utility. Indeed, the house was never meant to handle guests. "The idea is to spend time with our friends who live here. The house shifts the focus from having people *in* it to spending time *outside* of it," says the wife. Baker, now a ceramicist and sculptor in California, never misses a Maine summer—or dinner with his clients in the house he built. "If you love Maine, it's the glue that keeps you together," he says.

OPPOSITE: On the rare occasions when the family eats inside, a Parsons table and mismatched chairs does the trick. Minimal decoration keeps the emphasis on the view out the windows. ABOVE: Only essential furniture—much of it handed on from family—fills the cottage.

THE STONE HOUSE

• • •

Three thousand islands stretch up and down the coast of Maine, their names—Flapjack, Cow, Butter, Cabbage, and at least thirty named Little—as curious as their beauty is breathtaking. While on a consolation boat ride after selling their longtime summer house, Kate Horgan and her husband, Bob, spied a camp that appeared to spring from the rocks on an island in the distance. Overcome with seller's remorse, Horgan pulled out her phone and called a real estate agent immediately. Yes, it is for sale, and yes, the key is under the mat, and yes, let yourselves in. "It felt like being in a church," she says. "The walls are so thick, you can't really hear what's going on outside."

And there is so much going on outside. One acre at high tide, three at low, the tiny island is at the mercy of the open Atlantic. But for more than a century, the former hunting camp has absorbed the ocean's fury. "The first spring, we returned to find the front door

At sunset on this tiny island, the view is reflected in the windows spanning the west-facing side of the cottage.

and two kitchen windows gone. There was a boulder in the living room," says Horgan. It was the last time she shoveled a foot of sand and shells off the ground floor; in the ensuing years, the couple put on a tin roof, replaced the inherited plywood winter window coverings with boulder-proof polycarbonate, and rimmed the interior with a railing at cornice height from which to suspend their furniture in the off-season.

But the couple was careful to preserve the character that drew them to the house in the first place. They pointed the stones around the lichen growing on an exterior wall and built seating areas into the rocks. A sensitive interior renovation brought running water and electricity, as well as a bedroom and bathroom downstairs. But nothing has changed beyond the cottage's four walls. Fog socks it in, hurricanes knock at its door, and every sunset is the most glorious one ever. "Life revolves around the tide and the weather. We've had to rescue baby seals that get caught in the tidal pools. It's as close to nature as you can get," says Horgan.

ABOVE: With a ready oyster knife, a little rosé on hand, and a front yard full of oysters, cocktail hour is as good as it gets. OPPOSITE: The island is a five-minute motorboat ride from the mainland, followed by a long walk to shore on the deep-water dock.

OVERLEAF: Steel rods and hooks for hanging the furniture in the off-season rim the room just under the rafters.

HUNTING ISLAND

ABOVE: Nature provided the perfectly designed—and beautiful—banister. OPPOSITE: Horgan chose furnishings that would not compete with the raw beauty both inside and out.

ABOVE: The guesthouse straddles the best of two worlds: the ocean's edge and the woods.

•

RIGHT: The couple is never surprised to find the walls and seating areas reclaimed by the sea when they arrive each spring; rebuilding them is part of the beauty of island living.

•

OPPOSITE: Doors span almost the entirety of the ocean-side wall, allowing guests to turn the bedroom into a luxurious lean-to.

BERT ANDRÉ
MARQUET

THE BIG HOUSE

Jim Terry's earliest memory of traveling to the Big House, the summer cottage his maternal grandparents built in 1917, was when he was seven. On his paternal side, the expat Terry family had been living all over the world, and in 1939 they were in Holland, where they embarked on a boat to America as Hitler was invading Poland.

For the last four decades, Terry and his wife of sixty-five years, Maudie, have been the stewards of this ancestral home, where the century-old walls have absorbed the voices of six generations. And those walls! Terry's grandmother specified the stain herself—a mix of Prussian blue, yellow ochre, linseed oil, and turpentine—and it has remained untouched since.

Not that the Big House is precious. Its raw beauty was meant to slide seamlessly into its surroundings, a paean to the rusticators of the era. The nine bedrooms—among them the Pink Room, with its secret door to what was once the servants' quarters—were routinely filled with guests. The great room hummed with raucous dinners and music and art gatherings all summer long. "We would often show up to a full house. If you were lucky, you would get the cot in the nursery, but usually we would go off and camp on the nearby island," says Terry's daughter, Elizabeth.

The whole Terry family got involved in hand dipping and applying the gray shingles that cover the entire house.

ABOVE: Nooks throughout the house offer quiet spaces when family members want to take a break from gathering in the great room. OPPOSITE: The view from the second-floor sunset porch: the family cuddy cabin boat is anchored just off the deep-water dock.

That intrepid spirit was likely inherited. Jim and Maudie have never shrunk from the daunting task of preserving the Big House. "It has really shaped our lives. It was like joining the nunnery of Maine," says Jim, who was practicing law at the time. There was its jacking up: Jim armed with only belted khakis, pencils, a ladder, and a team of cousins to buttress the sagging house. There was the reshingling, with family enlisted to dip the cedar planks into paint before fastening them to the exterior. Maudie took care of the interior: stitching slip-covers and curtains, replacing mattresses, painting floors.

The couple's commitment to the Big House shows up inside and out, but for Elizabeth, it is the aural memories that have kept it alive for her. It is impossible to step onto the sun-set porch and not hear ice clinking in glasses, a cheese knife rattling on china, and the snap of Ritz crackers. "To me, the Big House has always been the crucible of my father's dreams—of family legacy, of public leadership, and of loving will. But it was my mother's valor and strength—over countless years of renovation and renewal—that has made this dream truly habitable for the rest of us."

USA
1000
PUZZLE
MAINE
USA
1000
PUZZLE

THE LOAVES AND FISHES COOKBOOK
BICENTENNIAL COOKBOOK

PRECEDING PAGES: Terry says the house pleases him most when there is music floating through it.

OPPOSITE: The "office" at the Big House consists of a rotary telephone and a wall-mounted pencil sharpener in the kitchen; who can work when the ocean beckons?

ABOVE: The kitchen has remained largely the same for more than fifty years.

CLOCKWISE FROM ABOVE LEFT: The Big House color palette was established from the start, springing from the stained walls in the great room: four different shades of blue-green in varying states of wear never seem to date. A table and benches tucked into the library serve as the children's corner and sometimes as a tea nook. Upstairs, the fir walls have remained raw since the cottage was built.

OPPOSITE: A turn-of-the-century rush chair belonging to Terry's grandparents has endured through six generations of quiet reading and nursing babies.

ABOVE: All nine bedrooms are named for a predominant color or motif: the green room for its painted floors, the blue room for its doors, the pink room for its cushions and curtains, and the bird room for an oil painting and the old crows on the curtains. OPPOSITE: A balcony, rimmed by bedrooms, overlooks the double-height great room.

A
LITTLE LAKE COTTAGE

• • •

Though it doesn't have an official name, the tiny camp that Polly Saltonstall and her husband, John Hanson, bought almost twenty years ago earned one soon after the closing. "It became immediately clear that the place needed far more work than we anticipated," says Saltonstall. Among family and friends, it became known as Polly's Folly.

What the three-bedroom cottage lacked in upkeep, it made up for in history. One of a cluster of former bathhouses for the Lake City Hotel, a late nineteenth-century pile that burned to the ground in the early 1900s, its most colorful owner, George Cleveland, ran the small excursion steamboat *Titwillow* on the lake. He also played cards with neighbors whose camps sometimes changed hands in poker games. The outbuilding, now a master bedroom, began life as a garage for a house in town.

Saltonstall drew up plans to expand the camp but never did. "Our job is to hew as close as possible to the original," she says.

"My goal was to preserve the feeling of the place, to take it back to its original charm," says Saltonstall. She furnished it the old-fashioned way: with family cast-offs, pieces found at estate sales, and local art. Instead of replacing the screen in the door, a friend mended it. Saltonstall preserved as much of the interior pine planking as she could and stained any replacements to match. Though it was too far gone to save, the kitchen looks as if it may have been redone in the 1950s, with a linoleum-like floor and Formica countertops. Honoring the past didn't stop with the interior, however. Cleveland had his poker, but Saltonstall prefers a different high-stakes pastime. Every autumn, she hosts Polly's Folly Fall Regatta on the sprawling lake just beyond her front door. Dozens enter in their kayaks, lasers, paddleboards, blue jays, and sailing dinghies. "I buy the prizes, never more than a dollar each, and I try to make sure everyone is a winner. One year, I found John Deere mugs on remainder. Those were a big hit."

ABOVE: Saltonstall replaced the Lilly Pulitzer upholstery on the horsehair sofa, a hand-me-down from her grandmother, with a pattern suited to lake life. OPPOSITE: A vintage sign from the fish hatchery where lake and river meet hangs just inside the front door.

MEGUNTICOOK
Lake
SALMON · BASS · TROUT
PICKEREL · PERCH
and GAME ASSOCIATION
MAINE

TROUT

Olympia Beer

PRECEDING PAGES: A room with a view; the double doors stay open all summer.

OPPOSITE: Maine artist Dan Falt carved the Megunticook White Fish, as Saltonstall affectionately calls it, from one piece of wood.

ABOVE: A rare solo canoe ride at sunset; the dock is a popular hangout all summer.

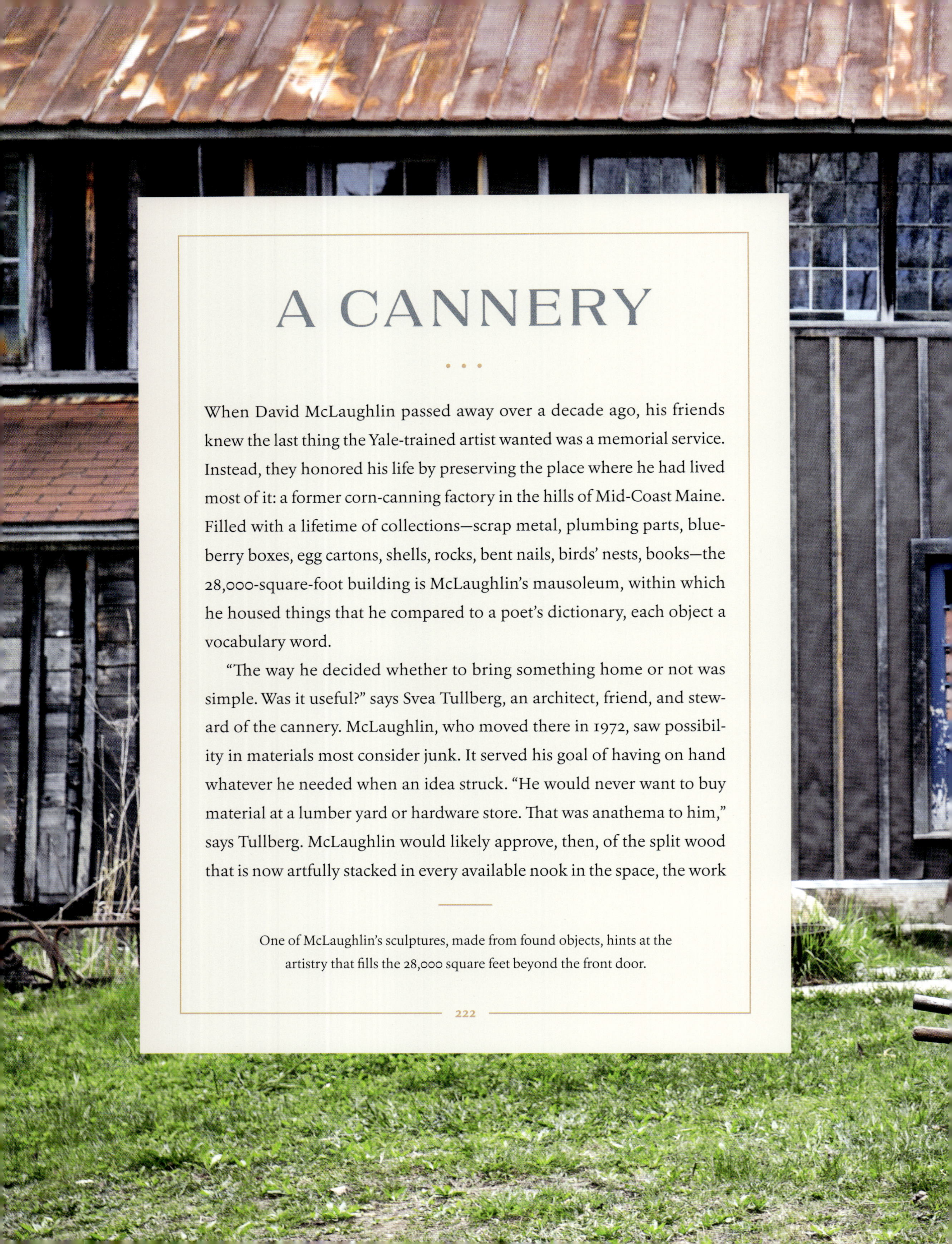

A CANNERY

When David McLaughlin passed away over a decade ago, his friends knew the last thing the Yale-trained artist wanted was a memorial service. Instead, they honored his life by preserving the place where he had lived most of it: a former corn-canning factory in the hills of Mid-Coast Maine. Filled with a lifetime of collections—scrap metal, plumbing parts, blueberry boxes, egg cartons, shells, rocks, bent nails, birds' nests, books—the 28,000-square-foot building is McLaughlin's mausoleum, within which he housed things that he compared to a poet's dictionary, each object a vocabulary word.

"The way he decided whether to bring something home or not was simple. Was it useful?" says Svea Tullberg, an architect, friend, and steward of the cannery. McLaughlin, who moved there in 1972, saw possibility in materials most consider junk. It served his goal of having on hand whatever he needed when an idea struck. "He would never want to buy material at a lumber yard or hardware store. That was anathema to him," says Tullberg. McLaughlin would likely approve, then, of the split wood that is now artfully stacked in every available nook in the space, the work

One of McLaughlin's sculptures, made from found objects, hints at the artistry that fills the 28,000 square feet beyond the front door.

of another steward, a local wood carver who watches over McLaughlin's life-size installation.

Friends point to a particular incident at Yale as seeding McLaughlin's passion for working with metals. "He needed to attach a fender to his motorcycle and found the equipment in the art department," says Tullberg. He started welding and never stopped. One of the thirty-six stoves McLaughlin built from the canning retorts he inherited when he bought the place sits proudly in the kitchen, a perfect symbol of its maker's talent for turning discarded materials into beautiful, useful objects. Tullberg, however, suspects that McLaughlin's resourcefulness was genetic. "He started collecting old tube radios as a kid, inspired by a box of pencils his mother refused to throw away," says Tullberg. "She labeled the container 'Pencils Too Short To Use.'"

OPPOSITE: In an homage to its original owner, the Cannery's current steward stacked wood around one of McLaughlin's signature light fixtures. ABOVE: The narrowest of spaces were fair game for collections; heart-shaped rocks are hard to resist.

AUBREY BEARDSLEY
MAINE COAST

OPPOSITE: Why restrict a black-and-white-checkerboard motif to the floor? Repeated on the table and apron of the narrow window shelf, the pattern brings visual order to a room filled with furniture, books, and objects.

ABOVE LEFT: McLaughlin found a use for the canning retorts—vessels into which the canning baskets were submerged—that were left behind. He made thirty-six wood-burning stoves, each one unique.

ABOVE RIGHT: He found a way to safely use knob-and-tube wiring to make a light fixture.

OVERLEAF LEFT: A granny-square crocheted quilt, garlands of dried marigolds, dried sunflowers and corn, a collection of sea urchins—it all has a place in McLaughlin's world.

OVERLEAF RIGHT: Firewood as sculpture: in the entrance, a pillar of artfully stacked kindling.

A CUSTOMS WAREHOUSE

• • •

It's hard to find the southern Maine that drew Corey Daniels to it permanently from upstate New York in 1979. The region of almost half a century ago was the essence of the cyclical and regenerative, before novelty and growth became more prized than stewardship and preservation. Daniels was an antiques dealer back then, and Maine provided. "There was really a rhythm to it. My dealer friends and I were buying and selling out of our cars, driving all over looking for things," he says.

All the while, he was searching for his own piece of this mythic place. Of the hauntingly beautiful island compound he now calls home, Daniels is matter-of-fact. "It was very, very rough when I bought it; then I fixed it up, and now it's rough again," he says. Fixing it up would suggest completion, but there is a dynamism in Daniels's approach. Several years ago, he shored up the tumbledown barn with a new foundation yet left the spartan interior largely intact. More recently, he tore off the ell that once housed the primary living spaces and is currently building a detached modernist house—smart, solar, and with triple-glazed windows—to replace it. "I always wanted to build a new house and not live in something that's old and demands attention all the time," he says with a laugh.

The former customs warehouse was moved a few hundred yards from its original site in the 1860s, when it was repurposed as a home.

But Daniels will always have a project in the late eighteenth-century building. The principal structure, a former customs warehouse and the oldest building on the island, remains on the tidal river where it was moved more than a century ago. Flooded with light and heaving with a half-century's worth of Daniels's idiosyncratic possessions, every room in the 50-foot-wide by 25-foot-deep space is a tableau vivant of the curator's philosophy. "I am drawn to beautiful design. I don't care about its worth," he says.

That would explain the sundry mix of furnishings and objects in the house's warren of Colonial-era rooms. In Daniels's hands, a block of wood, a barrister's chair, a tin box, a length of pitted chain look like a million bucks. But perhaps the starkest examples are found on the grounds: an outsized mooring ball appears as if it has come to rest under a tangle of bushes, and a series of granite posts stand sentry in an open field. "I bought them from a guy in New Hampshire because I liked them. Then I just had someone stick them in the ground," Daniels says.

ABOVE AND OPPOSITE: "I don't care who made it or how much it is worth. If I gravitate to it, then it is worth something to me. It could be an old hammer, a hunk of wood, or a bunch of metal frames. I think I have a little Marcel Duchamp in me," says Daniels.

OPPOSITE: An early twentieth-century bust of a boy that Daniels found in Amsterdam presides over an arrangement of objects prized for their patina; an empty frame is worth hanging simply for its shape and surface texture. ABOVE: The afternoon light casts particularly pleasing shadows throughout the house; it is the time Daniels likes best to take a walk through.

MÉLANGES
SONGS
BILITIS

PRECEDING PAGES: Daniels has been collecting for more than forty-five years. Shape, texture, patina—not provenance—drive his acquisitions. Orbs, columns, boxes, and vessels made from honest materials—marble, wood, metal, and ceramic—cover his desk. "It's nothing anyone would want, but I do have an affection for it all."

ABOVE: Orbs and chairs show up throughout Daniels's home, here arranged in a play of scale that highlights the heights of the window, door, and mantel.

OPPOSITE: Daniels converted the barn on the property into a studio with a view of the marsh where he takes his daily swims.

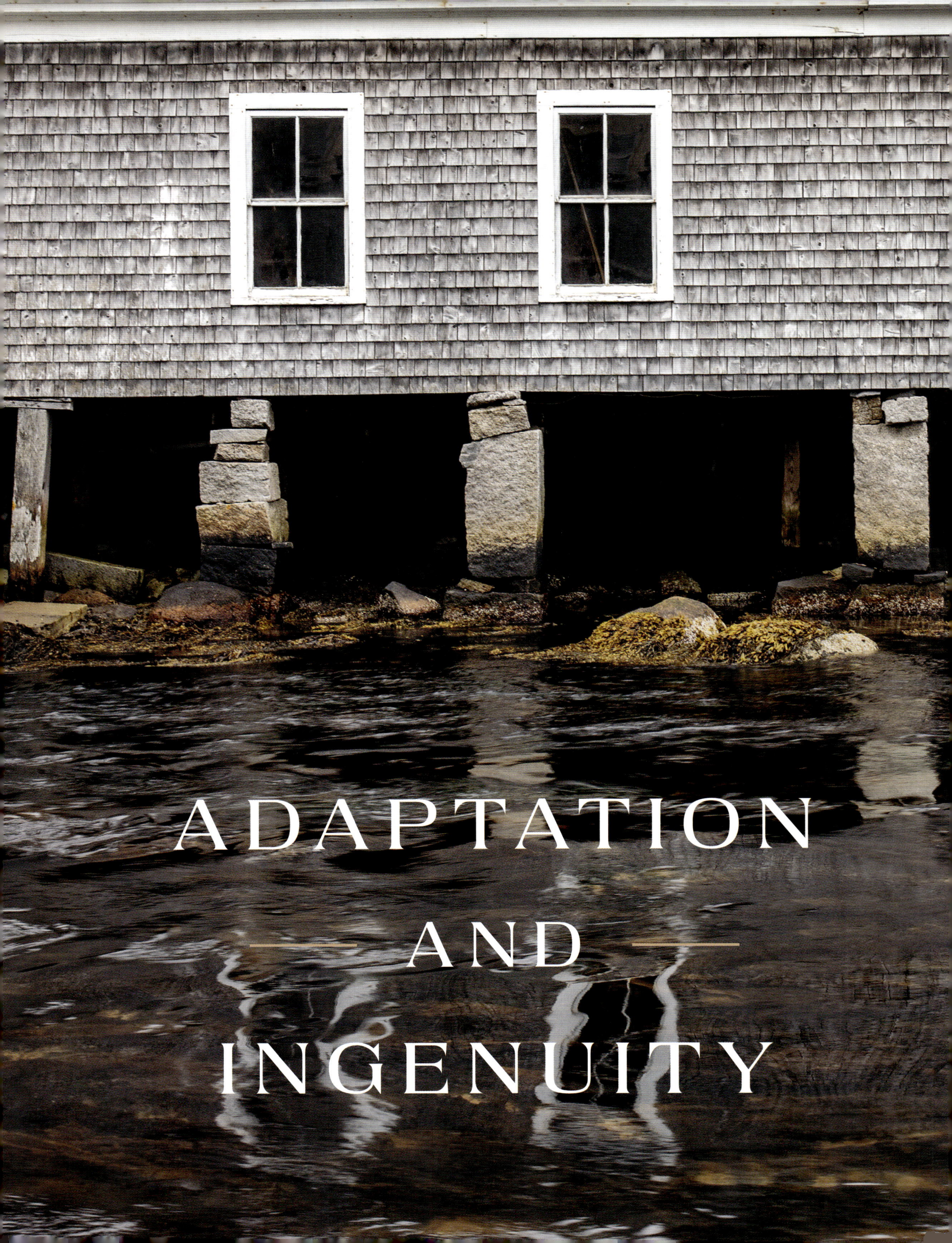

ADAPTATION AND INGENUITY

A CARRIAGE HOUSE

Until recently, there was a trapdoor under the dining table in the island carriage house that David Hopkins shares with artist David Wilson and their two Chinese crested powderpuffs. Its original purpose was, of course, to dispose of horse dung. But Hopkins found another use for it when he took up residence here forty years ago. "My nieces and nephews would throw table scraps through it and jig for squid. I can still hear their squeals of delight."

Hopkins, who spent three decades as a merchandiser at the Metropolitan Museum of Art, loved that hatch. "I'd rather live with layers of evidence of what has come before than in something cleaned and restored," he says. In the late 1990s, a storm surge burst open the trapdoor; as the water receded, it took some of the couple's favorite pieces of china—a reproduction asparagus vase among them—out to sea. To Hopkins's regret, that was the end of the hatch.

Still, much history remains in the 200-year-old building on Hopkins' Wharf, named for a great-grandfather who arrived on the island

"It's like living on a boat," says Hopkins. The changing light dances on the ceiling throughout the day.

Interwoven Globe
KANTHA
VANITY FAIR PORTRAITS
PARIS IN THE 1920s
ARMENIA
INDIA
LIFE AT THE TOP
cooking in the moment
TUCCI COOKBOOK
MAGRITTE A to Z
BEATRIX POTTER
COWGIRL CREAMERY
AGAINST the GRAIN

LEFT: Antique handline fishing reels were used for ice fishing on the ponds that dot the island.

OPPOSITE: The two-room—one up, one down—cottage rests entirely on pilings. The island's former icehouse sits just behind it.

in the late 1800s and founded an icehouse, grain shed, and general store. Phone numbers penciled on the wall, initials carved into beams and Great-aunt Eleanor's notes scribbled on the lumber used to repair the roof are as fixed as the granite pilings holding the place up. "We can read her handwriting as we go to sleep in the loft," says Hopkins of the second-floor space that also serves as Wilson's studio.

A reverence for patina fills every corner of the home: paintings by Wilson's Scottish grandfather and great-grandfather, piles of blue china Hopkins had reproduced while at the Met, his Auntie Hope's dining chairs, the dining table from his father, and a pedestal-turned-chopping block from impressionist Frank Benson's island studio. There's also that long-ago-lost asparagus vase, unearthed from the clam flats by a child playing under the house, aged to perfection by Mother Nature.

Hopkins jokes that every summer, tourists come wandering into the house, thinking it is an antiques shop. One of the most memorable was a gentleman from California who couldn't believe the Davids didn't live in fear of an earthquake. "I find that living here, in the place where my entire family has lived for centuries, has put me on a solid foundation. I feel safer here than anywhere."

CLOCKWISE FROM ABOVE LEFT: The chopping block between the stove and counter came from the studio of island artist Frank W. Benson. Some of the couple's beloved objects hang in between the studs. A ladder leads to Wilson's attic studio.

OPPOSITE: "It has nothing to do with decoration," says Hopkins of the interior. The dining table was handed down from his father and the harp-backed chairs from his Auntie Hope, who was the telephone operator for the island phone company that his grandfather owned.

A UNION HALL

Only an architect could have fallen for it. The century-old building, listing like a sailboat in a squall, was slowly sinking into the ground. It stood, if barely, on wet ground in the middle of the village, hard to ignore but easy to dismiss. It stopped Bruce Norelius in his tracks. "I found it delightfully awkward," he says. Perhaps suffering from an identity crisis, the ungainly eyesore was the town's original union hall. It was eventually turned into a high school and later became a publishing house. "It was a bit of a whale on the outside, but I loved it," says Norelius, who was practicing architecture in a nearby town at the time.

Moving house in Maine can mean many things, but a literal interpretation is historically not uncommon. So Norelius did what so many before him had done. He had the building picked up and moved to a sturdier plot, which happened to be next door. "There was a part of me that always wanted to live in a loft in a city. But when I moved to Maine I was hooked. To get to reuse an old building in a small village? It was too good to be true," says Norelius, who spent his early adult years in Seattle.

Drawn to both historical and contemporary architecture, Norelius used the 1,500-square-foot space to bring out the best in both. "It was my grand experiment," he says of the interior design. He tore away the ceiling—exposing the joists—to give the space texture and replaced the original floorboards with poured concrete. "The old floor was not practical, and I wanted a cooler, crisper surface underfoot," he says. Where steel columns might have gone, Norelius opted for a prefabricated wooden version that recall the Greek Revival architecture synonymous with New England. The kitchen, on the other hand, is a nod to the 1980s, the period when Norelius

Norelius was inspired by the work of architect John Pawson and artist Donald Judd; trimless windows and floors give the space a contemporary cool, yet he left the original ceiling joists exposed and installed traditional columns to hold it up.

KATSURA

PRECEDING PAGES: The symmetrical arrangement of furniture—the Adirondack chairs by Maine-based Cold Mountain Builders are based on a 1920s design—infuses the room with calm.

•

LEFT: Slick poured-concrete floors reflect the natural light that fills the space.

RIGHT: Utilitarian cabinets set on casters provide storage for the entire space; clothes, dishes, books, and linens are all hidden behind closed doors.

•

OPPOSITE: Norelius is reluctant to change the graphic kitchen cabinets—a nod to the 1980s, when he studied architecture.

studied architecture. “I try not to let that sensibility come out too much, and though my impulse is to change it, I hesitate because it *is* a particular era,” he says.

A move to the West Coast with partner Landis Green, a school headmaster whom Norelius met two decades ago in Maine, means that the pair spends their summers in the former union hall. “There is a wonderful calm here that keeps us coming back,” says Norelius. And so do neighbors, who knock on the door at all times of day. “We love the spontaneity. It’s like living in another time.”

LITTLE PEEK

• • •

When Maria Berman and Brad Horn, founders of the New York City–based architectural firm Berman Horn Studio, first visited Maine, they stayed on an island in a rented house that was entirely off the grid. "It was the most relaxing vacation *ever*," says Berman. Smitten, as so many first-time visitors are, they continued renting a cottage every summer, all the while searching for a piece of land. It would be three years after finding the perfect spot—an expanse of farmland strewn with conifers, huckleberry brambles, and bay laurel perched high above a tranquil cove—that the couple would move into their modernist idyll, named for the glimpses of it from the water.

Known for reaching into the past to inform their work, Berman and Horn practiced what they preached. Before producing a single drawing, they built a road to the property and visited it over the course of several months to determine how best to site the house. "We were lucky to be able to build it with only a charming fisherman's cottage in view," says Berman. At the same time, they traveled the New England coast, landing on the Jethro Coffin house, a Cape and the oldest house on Nantucket, as well as the John Whipple house, a saltbox, in Ipswich, Massachusetts, as their references. "We loved the severity of them, that they are not so big and muscular. Yet they were built to endure," she says.

The pair viewed the historic houses through a modernist lens, expanding the windows and raising the ceiling to create a twenty-first-century

Maria Berman and Brad Horn fell in love with the alpine landscape—the result of acidic, shallow soil—that surrounds Little Peek.

ABOVE: The couple took inspiration from the tradition of painted surfaces that defines old New England homes, adding a touch of gloss so that the floor reflects all of that glorious light. OPPOSITE: A hallmark of New England summer cottages, a wicker chair in the gleaming master bedroom reads as sculpture.

version of its colonial forebears. "Those houses were built to shelter from the harsh weather, with tiny windows and low ceilings. We shifted the scale to achieve a lighter, brighter interior," says Berman.

The couple, however, largely looked outside to make the most important decisions. The screened porch, flanked by the main house and the guesthouse, allows for seeing through the structure to the land, air, and sea. "When you find a site you love and you build a house on it, it irrevocably changes that site," says Berman. To that end, they bathed the interiors in bright white paint, all the better to focus on the view beyond. Sparsely furnished in a smattering of styles—some Americana, a little bit of Memphis, a touch of pop, and a whiff of flea market—the interior works hard not to compete. Striking that balance is an ongoing effort, as it is in the couple's life itself. "Being here is so incredibly precious to me. To have this conceptual break and physical break—it becomes real as soon as the ferry leaves the mainland."

Berenice Abbott
American Photographer
by Hank O'Neal
Commentary by Berenice Abbott
River Cafe London

PRECEDING PAGES: A little bit of Americana, a little bit of Memphis: the couple filled the interior with pieces that strike a balance between the two styles.

ABOVE: The door to the guest cottage quietly blends into the shingled exterior.

LEFT: A screened porch redefined: centering it allows for seeing "through" the house.

OPPOSITE: Berman, who is also an art conservator with a specialty in textiles, uses them to inject color into the guest bedroom.

Chestnut Sided Warbler

A HOUSE OVER THE SHOP

• • •

"Maine chooses you," says Sharon Mrozinski, one half of the thirty-year partnership—in life and work—that is the Marston House. Together with her husband, Paul, she has built an international clientele of interior designers and devotees of the vintage French linens, silver, furnishings, and *objets* that bear the hallmarks of the pair's adopted home state—and the couple themselves: grit, soul, and enduring beauty.

Vision, too, is innate to the Mrozinskis. "Isn't it magical?" waxed Paul when he first stood in front of the building they now call home. "It's chaos," wailed Sharon, as she took in her tumbledown surroundings. His was a faraway gaze—out to the storybook working harbor, the majestic osprey nest, and the bobbing lobster boats. Hers zoomed in closer. "The space was so ugly and it smelled," she recalls.

But not for long. The early nineteenth-century clapboard building, once the post office on a neighboring island, had been moved to this one by boat in 1906 and recycled countless times, into a paper goods shop, a gas station, and a dry goods store.

Birds, nests, and eggs show up everywhere in the Mrozinskis' lives, as in this early American cupboard.

Paul, a trained architect, recycled it yet again, into a street-level shop and second-floor living space that is as honest in its beauty as the harbor view from their bedroom window.

Home is their Crow's Nest, affectionately named for the building's siting at a bend in the main street, which affords a view of the village's comings and goings in both directions. Upstairs is downstairs come to life, a tableau vivant of the Mrozinskis' shared aesthetic, filled as it is with furnishings and textiles that grow more beautiful with age.

Indeed, time turned Sharon around. On the day she and Paul first saw the property, they walked into a nearby shop. The proprietor, noting the defeat on Paul's face, handed him a key to an apartment upstairs and told the pair to stay as long as they needed. "I will never forget how she looked us in the eyes and said, 'Don't lose the magic,'" says Sharon. "All of the things I love about Maine were distilled in those early days."

ABOVE: Bookshelves provide precious real estate: the couple reserve them for their favorite books and objects collected since they met in the early 1980s. OPPOSITE: An early taxidermy goose, birds'-egg lithographs, and boxed collections of eggs command a corner of the bedroom.

OVERLEAF: The kitchen décor brings to life the offerings in the shop downstairs.

ABOVE: A charcoal of a crow by Franna Lusson watches over Paul's office, which doubles as the entrance—by apple ladder—to the attic. OPPOSITE: Guests are treated to luxe camp-style quarters in the attic, where cots are fitted out with downy duvets and homespun linen.

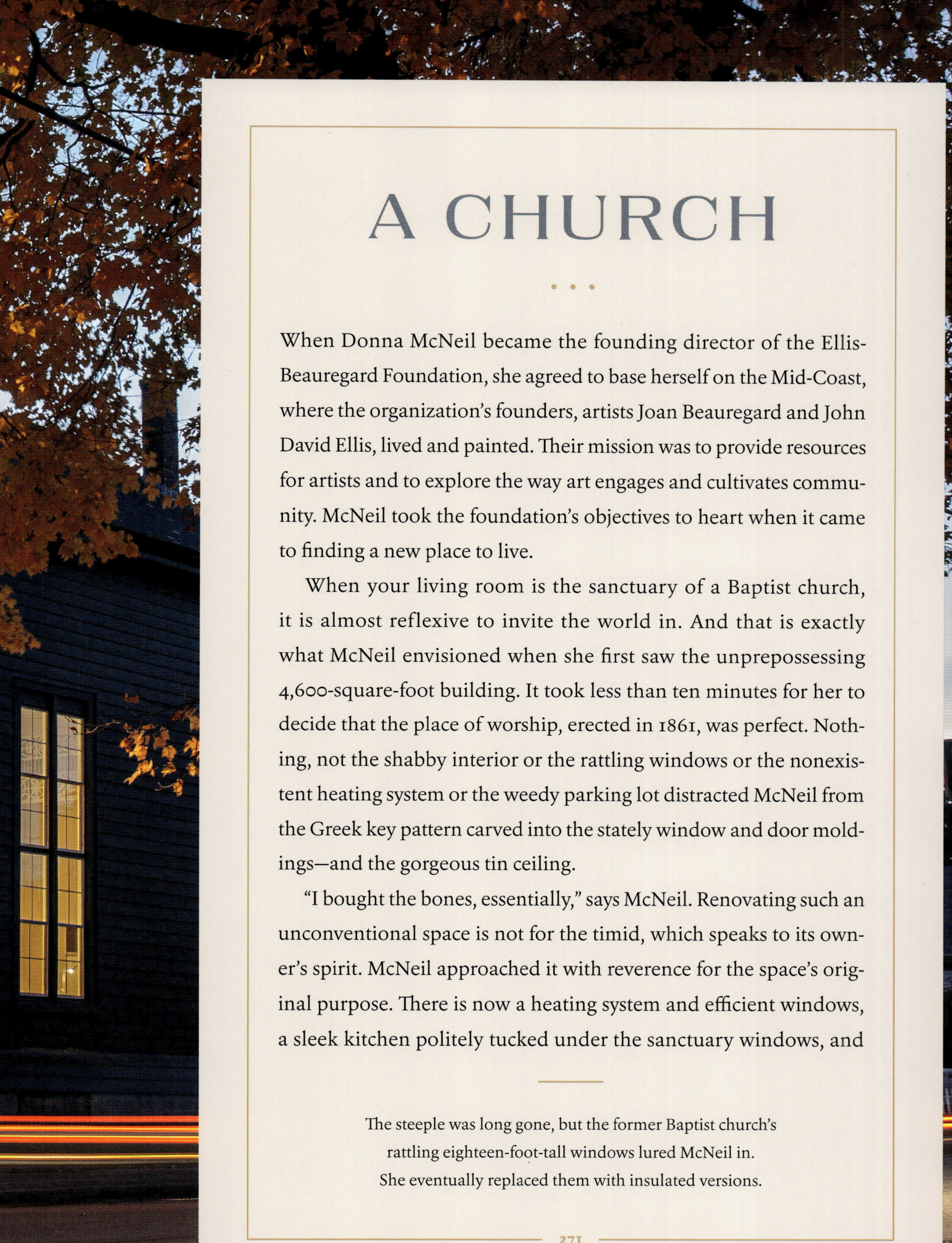

A CHURCH

• • •

When Donna McNeil became the founding director of the Ellis-Beauregard Foundation, she agreed to base herself on the Mid-Coast, where the organization's founders, artists Joan Beauregard and John David Ellis, lived and painted. Their mission was to provide resources for artists and to explore the way art engages and cultivates community. McNeil took the foundation's objectives to heart when it came to finding a new place to live.

When your living room is the sanctuary of a Baptist church, it is almost reflexive to invite the world in. And that is exactly what McNeil envisioned when she first saw the unprepossessing 4,600-square-foot building. It took less than ten minutes for her to decide that the place of worship, erected in 1861, was perfect. Nothing, not the shabby interior or the rattling windows or the nonexistent heating system or the weedy parking lot distracted McNeil from the Greek key pattern carved into the stately window and door moldings—and the gorgeous tin ceiling.

"I bought the bones, essentially," says McNeil. Renovating such an unconventional space is not for the timid, which speaks to its owner's spirit. McNeil approached it with reverence for the space's original purpose. There is now a heating system and efficient windows, a sleek kitchen politely tucked under the sanctuary windows, and

The steeple was long gone, but the former Baptist church's rattling eighteen-foot-tall windows lured McNeil in. She eventually replaced them with insulated versions.

OPPOSITE AND LEFT: The narthex has become a stage, though the act of cooking and eating in the vast space can feel like performance in itself.

upstairs, a new bathroom and four sparsely furnished bedrooms. The abandoned parking lot is now a lush garden. It's all so striking and, when one considers the siding-clad exterior McNeil painted onyx, unlike any other Baptist church anywhere.

"So many people came by when I finished renovating it to tell me that they almost bought it," says McNeil. Not one to become undone by the What ifs?, McNeil allows those questions to mobilize, rather than paralyze, her. "I'm just foolish enough," she says. And that seems to have charmed the community. Though the soaring space's eighteen-foot windows make it a challenge to stage art openings, McNeil's home has become a lively meeting place for community dinners, art talks, and music and dance performances.

"In a way, it is a grand folly," says McNeil. "But you know, I wake up every day and stand at the choir loft and sing. It gives you the most expansive heart. Because it is a 40-foot-by-40-foot space, you, too, become wide open. This place doesn't confine my spirit."

CLOCKWISE FROM LEFT: A Donald Judd–inspired bed floats in the middle of a guest bedroom. A mix of traditional and contemporary pieces brings out the beauty in each. All-white walls put a spotlight on a painted iron bed and the visual rhyme it makes with the plants at its foot.

OPPOSITE: McNeil has always lived in sparsely decorated homes, but such a voluminous space pushed her minimalist leanings to the extreme; the few furnishings appear to float.

TWO FARMETTES

• • •

When Tony Elliott was a kid, his Christmas lists would include things like toy farm sets and horses, live birds, and gardening tools. "One of the farm sets came with grass that actually grew, so I could pretend the horses were eating it," says Elliott, who grew up in the Midwest. As a teenager, he designed a formal garden with a birdbath and a walkway in the center. In college, where he studied agronomy, he kept parakeets in his dorm room.

At Snug Harbor Farm in southern Maine, miniature pinto horses eat real grass (and hay). Old English, Golden Sebright, and Silkie chickens roost in a coop. Frillback pigeons live in a dovecote near greenhouses filled with topiaries, succulents, and ferns. And an aptly named pied peacock presides over it all.

Ever since he spied the FOR SALE sign in front of the ailing farm twenty years ago, every day has been Christmas for Elliott. Originally the home of a retired sea captain, the tiny 1850s Cape with its attached barn, milking shed, and smattering of outbuildings has become the place where the landscape designer has brought his childhood wish list to life. "A farmette, a nursery, growing fields, and a shop where his topiaries, garden statuary, and "cool plants in cool pots" have been draws for years, cover three acres.

Don't ask Tony Elliott how many chickens he has; one of them, an Old English breed, flees the coop at Snug Harbor Farm.

ABOVE AND OPPOSITE: Elliott, who was raised Catholic, christened one building the DeVine shop for the vines growing all over it. He prunes the hedges to mimic flying buttresses. Inside, he stores the terra-cotta pots that he sells and that have become synonymous with Snug Harbor Farm.

Snug Harbor Farm is ever changing—its first inhabitants were a quintet of mixed-breed sheep that Elliott named the Jackson 5—with art shows, workshops, and, of course, a New England–style Christmas. But perhaps the most dramatic shift came just after Elliott found a customer using his bathroom. It was then he realized that his live/work arrangement needed some rethinking. Expanding his life to include another piece of property presented another dilemma, however: this admitted pet hoarder worried it would just become another place to populate with his beloved animals.

So Elliott made a deal with himself. He could purchase Ward Brook Farm, a classic little house, big house, back house, and barn, if he returned it to its working roots. He could raise animals, but they couldn't be simply for his own pleasure; the animals had to provide. Today, the barn is abuzz with Suffolk sheep, chickens, and laying hens and ducks.

It's a magical place, and Elliott would agree that it took a certain kind of magic to transform the sprawling property, built in the early 1700s, which had been left to deteriorate for

67 BAILEY ST.

CLOCKWISE FROM ABOVE LEFT: A gem-studded glass pendant from India illuminates an inherited early American portrait. The frillback pigeons at Snug Harbor Farm are a current obsession in a lifetime of fascination with birds. Floorboards repurposed from the barn complement the raw walls in a bedroom.

OPPOSITE: Elliott does not adhere to any particular design ethos; he fills his homes with things he wants to look at, many of them acquired on his travels.

decades by its previous owners. Over the last fifteen years, he has imbued the house with the Japanese aesthetic of *wabi-sabi*, an embrace of the impermanent and the imperfect. He hired two rough- rather than fine-finish carpenters because he wanted the rooms to look raw, as they might if they had aged well. He tore out the hayloft and attic floors and installed them throughout the living spaces. He played with the scale of the wainscoting in the kitchen and the trim around the windows. He didn't touch the old doors and worn walls in the blue bedroom upstairs.

As he does at Snug Harbor Farm, Elliott has endeavored to make Ward Brook Farm a genuine, honest place. "Does the isolation of living in Maine make it more genuine? I don't know that answer," he says. The pet lover part of him plays fast and loose with the honest part when it comes to his chickens. "When people ask me how many chickens I have, I say twelve. It is a total lie. I am not counting chickens."

ABOVE: Indian textiles adorn the windows; between them is a framed poster of Camille Claudel snagged from a lamppost in Brussels. OPPOSITE: In the travel room, an artist's drawing figure wearing an antique Chinese falconry helmet is mounted on an Indonesian pedestal.

OPPOSITE: Kiwi and white multiflora rose vines gone wild on the DeVine shop. ABOVE: Elliot left the stairway as he found it, painted with a faux-granite finish.

A FAMILY CAMPGROUND

• • •

Jennifer Kindig and Brad Clark had known each other for only six weeks when they fell in love. Though both would submit that they were smitten with each other, the object of their shared affections was a tiny cottage on a finger of land Down East. "We stood on the property and decided right then and there that we should buy it," says Kindig. "And I secretly thought how amazing it would be if the relationship worked out, and how awful it would be if it didn't."

Almost two decades and two children later, Kindig and Clark are still in love—with each other and with the property that their friends christened the Love Shack. Indeed, its previous owners spent forty summers there without running water or electricity. "They came back every summer for the first ten years to sit and look at the view, always relieved to find we hadn't changed anything," says Kindig, a third-generation antiques dealer and textiles obsessive.

It would have been easy for Kindig and Clark to build a proper house on the property, but they have resisted the impulse that afflicts so many

A sunburst inspired by design icon Tony Duquette marks the pitch of the barn, the most recent addition to the property.

ABOVE AND OPPOSITE: Though she deals in eighteenth-century American antiques, Kindig prefers to surround herself with the fruits of her travels. Southeast Asia, India, and Morocco are favorite destinations, as is evident throughout the barn.

who lose sight of why they fall in love with Maine in the first place. A pair of tent platforms seemed appropriate. "They remind me of summer camp," says Kindig. Albeit one done up in global nomadic style. Intrepid world travelers, this is a family that knows how to get comfortable in any setting. "The babies slept in cribs in the tents and we bathed them in lobster pots," says Kindig. Ten years in, they built a bathhouse—a guest room, bathroom, and office—with a fixed roof and walls and a tented front. The barn followed several years later. "Each time we add something, we convince ourselves we don't need a real house," says Kindig. Because, in truth, it's what's beyond four walls that keeps them there. "We joke about how many photos I take of our little point. I text one to my neighbor almost every day. And she texts back, 'I can see the same view from here.'"

ABOVE, LEFT, AND OPPOSITE: The Love Shack, the original building on the property, was named for the spell it cast on Kindig and Clark when they first saw it. They have left it exactly how they found it more than twenty years ago but furnished it with pieces collected over dozens of trips abroad.

OPPOSITE: Roughing it never looked so good: one of two furnished tents on the property that are open to guests all summer long. ABOVE: Every coastal house in Maine, from shack to château, must have an outdoor shower.

To Jim and Dot Walsh, my maternal grandparents,
who gave Maine to me and my family.

M.M.

For Peter and Henry, of course.

B.B.

For Aunt P., my ballast.

K.H.

ACKNOWLEDGMENTS

Thank you, first and foremost, to my daughter, Oona, for her unwavering support always. And to my sister, Mary Carmel, who was there with me in unheated cottages during the winter to get the shot. I owe so much to my parents, who made Maine their home and kept that fire burning in us all. —M.M.

To my parents, Judith and Brian, who gave me my Maine roots, and the rest of my dear family, who share them with me. And to the Fosters for showing me the meaning of a real summer cottage, alive with kids and grandparents and everyone in between. And to M. for asking me along on this adventure. —B.B.

As in everything, Stephen, Finn, and James make for the best Maine memories. Thank you. And to Tom, Mary Ann, Mary Jane, and Thomas Young (and Tommy and Daisy), who have cultivated in us a thirst for sailing the sea. What a gift. —K.H.

And from the three of us:

For their generous spirit, open hearts and open doors, we are grateful to the homeowners in these pages, especially Donna, Bill, Bruce, Polly, Sharon, and Jordana, who let us swim in their coves (and provided towels!), paddle their canoes to get that sunset shot, sleep in their guest rooms (under luxurious French duvets), borrow their cars (some antique), pester their friends, drink their espresso, eat their oysters, and drink their rosé. Oh, and thank you for trusting us to return the key to its hiding spot.

Carla Glasser is the best agent. That's all there is to say about that. To our friends at Vendome—publisher Mark Magowan, who was always supportive of his Maine Gang; Nina Magowan, for stepping in at exactly the right moment; editor Jackie Decter, whose enthusiasm was only matched by her gimlet eye; designer Mark Melnick, who displayed patience, perseverance, and talent in equal measure; Meghan Phillips, who got the word out; and Jim Spivey, who expertly shepherded the book through production—a heartfelt thank you. And to photographer, mentor, friend, and generally wonderful human William Abranowicz, for leading us to Vendome.

THE MAINE HOUSE
First published in 2021 by The Vendome Press
Vendome is a registered trademark of The Vendome Press LLC

VENDOME PRESS US
PO Box 566
Palm Beach, FL 33480

VENDOME PRESS UK
Worlds End Studio
132–134 Lots Road
London SW10 0RJ

www.vendomepress.com

ISBN 978-0-86565-394-8

PUBLISHERS Beatrice Vincenzini, Mark Magowan, and Francesco Venturi
EDITOR Jacqueline Decter
PRODUCTION DIRECTOR Jim Spivey
DESIGNER Mark Melnick

Library of Congress Cataloging-in-Publication Data available upon request

Distributed in North America by
Abrams Books
www.abramsbooks.com

Distributed in the rest of the world by
Thames & Hudson Ltd.
6–24 Britannia Street
London WC1X 9JD
United Kingdom
www.thamesandhudson.com

EU Authorized Representative
Interart S.A.R.L.
19 Rue Charles Auray
93500 Pantin, Paris
France
productsafety@vendomepress.com
www.interart.fr

Printed and bound in China

Printed on paper sourced and verified in compliance with the European Union Deforestation Regulation (EUDR).

SIXTH PRINTING

PAGE 1: A stone fireplace warms the side porch of the Big House (see pages 202–13).

PAGES 2–3: Corey Daniel's converted customs house in southern Maine (see pages 230–39).

PAGES 4–5: Dawn, as seen from E. B. White's dock (see pages 142–49).

PAGES 6–7: The view from Stone House, the sole structure on a Mid-Coast island (see pages 192–201).

PAGES 8–9: The High Head lighthouse (see pages 70–81).

PAGES 10–11: The Kennebunkport Yacht Club.

PAGES 12–13: The path E. B. White walked every day to his writing shack (see pages 142–49).

PAGE 294: One of dozens of protected harbors that draw sailors from all over the world to the coast of Maine.